Praise for
Ancient Egypt's Lord c

"*Anubis—Ancient Egypt's Lord of Death and Protection* explores the many roles Anubis played in the culture of ancient Egypt—from a god of mummification to heroic defender of the dead. Equal parts spirituality and history, this book provides a thorough explanation of the Anubis mythos punctuated by the author's own spiritual insights. Charlie Larson brings the worship of Anubis into the modern era with practical Egyptian magic and spell work for almost any occasion."

—Travis McHenry, author of the *Egyptian Star Oracle*

"This book is a deep, delicious swim in the darkness of the Egyptian underworld as personified by Anubis, wise Lord of the Afterlife. Compelling and extensive, written by a priest and true devotée working from direct personal knowledge as well as extensive research, this book ably brings into light the secrets and mysteries of Anubis and how they manifest through all the worlds, ancient, modern, and inner."

—deTraci Regula, author of *The Mysteries of Isis,*
Egyptian Scarab Oracle, and other works

"In his brilliant book *Anubis—Ancient Egypt's Lord of Death and Protection*, Charlie Larson takes us on a poignant, powerful, inclusive, and deeply personal journey to meet the Great God Anubis. Filled with solid historical information, as well as practical contemporary rituals, magick, healing practices and prayers, this book drew me in, opened my heart, and made me love dear Anubis even more."

—Michael Butler Smith, author of *Embracing Isis:*
A Witch's Guide to the Great Goddess

"Charlie Larson's elegant prose results in an approachable text that deftly guides those who seek to form a personal relationship with Anubis. A gifted teacher, Larson condenses what he's learned from his decades of research concerning the practices of ancient Anubites and suggests modern ways to connect with this mysterious Lord of Death. *Anubis—Ancient*

Egypt's Lord of Death and Protection is a unique and useful addition to any discerning reader's bookshelf."

—Martha Kirby Capo, author of *Thrifty Witchery*

"I love Charlie Larson's *Anubis*. Charlie does an excellent job of explaining the relationship of Anubis to those who are drawn to him and to those who consider themselves his children."

—Rev. NiankhSekhmet, owner of Alchemia Magic and priestess of Sekhmet at Nekhen Iunen Sekhmet (Shrine of Sekhmet's Sanctuary)

ANUBIS

Ancient Egypt's Lord
of Death and Protection

ANUBIS

Ancient Egypt's Lord
of Death and Protection

CHARLIE LARSON

Foreword by Jason Miller

WEISER
BOOKS

This edition first published in 2024 by Weiser Books,
an imprint of Red Wheel/Weiser, LLC
With offices at:
65 Parker Street, Suite 7
Newburyport, MA 01950
www.redwheelweiser.com

ISBN: 978-1-57863-841-3
Library of Congress Cataloging-in-Publication Data

Names: Larson, Charlie (Neopagan), author. | Miller, Jason, 1972- writer of foreword.
| Miller, Jason, 1972- other. Title: Anubis : ancient Egypt's lord of death and protection
/ Charlie Larson ; foreword by Jason Miller. Description: Newburyport, MA : Weiser
Books, 2024. | Includes bibliographical references. | Summary: "Portrayed as either a
black jackal or as a jackal-headed man, Anubis is Egypt's original Lord of the Dead. Even
after that title was eventually transferred to Osiris, Anubis continued to be the most active
participant in the after-death process, and this book focuses the spotlight squarely on him
and his various facets"-- Provided by publisher. Identifiers: LCCN 2024033129 | .
ISBN 9781578638413 (trade paperback) | ISBN 9781633413382 (ebook) Subjects:
LCSH: Anubis (Egyptian deity) | Kemeticism. | Spiritual life. | Magic. | BISAC: BODY,
MIND & SPIRIT / Occultism | HISTORY / Ancient / Egypt Classification: LCC BL2450.
A62 L37 2024 | DDC 299/.312113--dc23/eng20240805
LC record available at https://lccn.loc.gov/2024033129

Cover and interior by Sky Peck Design
Credits and information for interior photos/images on page 204.
Typeset in Sabon

Printed in the United States of America
IBI
10 9 8 7 6 5 4 3 2 1

Dedication

*For my dearest Anubis, Master of Mysteries and Lord of Transformation,
for all you've done in my life, I dedicate this book to you.*

Anubis—Anpu,
Jackal-headed One,
Liminal Lord,
Light in the Darkness,
Cosmic Balancer,
Lord of the Dead,
Sovereign of the Underworld,
Guide in the Afterlife,
God of Death,
Protector of Souls,
Obsidian Lord,
Master Shaman,
Navigator through Chaos,
Guide to the Lost,
Accounter of Hearts,
Opener of Ways,
Upholder of Ma'at,
God of Magick,
Master of Mystery,
Keeper of Keys,
Lord of the Shadows,
Healer of Souls,
You are my guide.
With you at my side
I find my strength.

Contents

Acknowledgments

There are so many people who have influenced me throughout my lifetime, and each and every person I have met along the way has helped to shape who I am today in one way or another. There are, however, a few people in particular that I'd like to mention.

Heartfelt thanks to my grandfather—my father figure—who taught me so many things about the natural world around us. He showed me how to listen to the whispers of the trees and the songs of birds. His wisdom of the unseen and unknown became the foundation for my spiritual practices today. Without knowing it, he, in his own way, led me to Anubis those many years ago. I will carry his love and guidance with me wherever I go.

To my partner, thank you for teaching me the true meaning of love and for helping show me my own worth. Thank you for encouraging me and pushing me to be the best version of myself that I can be. To my dear friend Neil, who embodied the meaning of strength and perseverance when times got hard—a lesson I will always remember—I honor your memory. To Samantha and Kayla, you are always my closest friends, no matter how near or far apart we are. I love you dearly. To my soul siblings, Kee and Serendipity, I thank you for being my "littermates" and dearest spiritual companions. To the many wonderful witches and Pagans I've met over the years on various social-media platforms, I love you all dearly and am grateful to have you in my life.

To Jason Mankey, I thank you for giving me the chance many years ago to write publicly on *The Agora*. Without that opportunity, I would never have been brave enough to put myself out there, and I wouldn't have realized how much I enjoy writing. And to Martha Kirby Capo, thank you for always giving me a place to continue my writing.

To my editor Judika Illes, thank you from the bottom of my heart for giving me the opportunity to share this book with the world. I am grateful for your wisdom, your guidance, and your words of encouragement. I admire you greatly.

And to Anubis, to whom I dedicate this book, there are no words for the multitude of ways in which you have touched my life and changed it for the better. Through ups and downs, you are always with me as the Liminal Lord, Great Guardian, and Lord of Transformation.

Foreword

I am writing this foreword from a hospital room, recovering from one surgery and awaiting another. Everything went as hoped and, unless something unusual happens, I will be fine. The guy in the bed next to me didn't fare as well. He came in with some bone pain and just found out he has weeks to live. As I sit here considering what to write about this book, he is getting his finances in order and breaking the bad news to his friends and family.

The presence of Anubis—Great Protector, Weigher of Souls, and Lord of Death—is palpable in this place.

Death is one of the few constants that bind us together. Every being ever born, from ancient Egypt to present-day America, dies. The universal mystery of death and what lies beyond is one of the first things that drew human attention to the world of spirit. For humans, at least, the indisputable fact of death seems to be accompanied by a sneaking suspicion that we continue to live on in some fashion.

Some of us simply seek comfort in the face of the unknown. Some want guidance about how to live in a way that ensures a good afterlife. Some long for a gnostic peek beyond the physical while they are still alive, while others, not satisfied with a peek, hunger for actual contact with powers they can petition and negotiate with, not only for a good death, but for a good life as well.

Anubis is one such power.

This book takes a deep dive into the history, mystery, and magic of Anubis, one that bridges the gap between the Nile Valley of 3000 BCE and wherever and whenever you happen to be reading it. Charlie Larson invites us to cross that bridge, and gives us the tools we need to do so.

Many of the Pagan books I was raised on went wide rather than deep when it came to deities and spirits. I have attended workshops where participants chanted the names of goddesses as if they were all just different versions of the same being. Isis, Astarte, Diana, Hekate, Demeter, and Kali were all thrown into a blender that yielded a bland "spirit smoothie." Even today, students ask me if Hekate, a goddess to whom I have dedicated decades, isn't the same as Kali, Santa Muerte, and the Morrigan, since they are all "Dark Goddesses."

Thankfully, there are a host of newer books written by teachers who are fighting this tendency, delving deeper into the mysteries of a single deity. This is the first such book that I have seen on Anubis, and I am thankful to have it.

This is not to say that deities don't overlap or are never synchronous. Charlie does an excellent job of showing how the Greeks syncretized Anubis with Hermes to create Hermanubis, a deity worshipped during the Ptolemaic period and mentioned in alchemical and magical texts up through the Renaissance. Hermanubis, in turn, influenced early depictions of Saint Christopher, the saint of travelers, who was portrayed early on with the head of a dog. Does this mean that they are necessarily the same deities with different faces? Or does it essentially signal the birth of a new being? For me, the answer is: Yes, no, both, and neither. Given how subtle we humans can be, I expect vast spiritual powers can be even more subtle and hard to nail down. Thus the mystery!

Works like this are hard to get right. They have to be rooted in history, but not get trapped in recreating a cult that is no longer relevant to the time and place in which we live. As Charlie notes, we no longer mummify the dead, nor do we entomb them with all their riches. Just as devotion to Anubis changed in Egypt over the 3,000 years before the Common Era, it is only natural for it to have changed over the 2,000 years between then and now. And it will change over the next 2,000 years as well.

In order for our practices to be relevant to our time and place, we need to establish fresh communications with the world of spirit. Of course, this has its risks. There is no shortage of Pagans who report having received messages and visions from the gods—commonly called UPG (Unverified Personal Gnosis). The quality of these communications varies widely, some descending to the level of personal fantasy or messages that are at odds with culture, with history, and with tradition. Unfortunately, these can disconnect us from spirit as much as they connect us. It requires a good deal of discernment to evaluate revelations from spirit in order to ensure that they are meaningful and actionable.

But when these two poles of research and revelation are handled with respect and insight, something magical happens. They do more than just co-exist; they harmonize and support each other. I am happy to say that this book does just that. It gives you the tools you need to make research and revelation rhyme.

I won't keep you any longer. You have a book to read and I am still in a hospital. Luckily, I will be released soon so that I can get on with my life. Thanks to this book, I hope to go about that with more of Anubis's wisdom under my belt, so that, when the time comes, I will meet him with a heart lighter than a feather.

May you do the same.

—Jason Miller, April 2024

Introduction

The day I first encountered Anubis began as just another nature adventure with my grandfather. It was a pretty regular occurrence for us to go hiking in the woods, watching birds and wildlife, looking for arrowheads out in the field, or simply driving around the countryside to see if we could find anything interesting. Even though I was only about five years old at the time, I can still remember many of the details of that day as if it were a realistic painting that has been pristinely preserved and cared for in a museum.

It was a sunny autumn day in Indiana. The air was crisp and cool, but it was warm enough to spend time outdoors. There was a chance of rain, but the clouds still appeared to be far to the west. Many of the leaves had already fallen, but some of the trees were still holding out for one last colorful hoorah before the winter months ahead. The corn and soybean crops had already been harvested, leaving a view of the landscape for miles and miles.

This particular day, we chose a wooded site just a few miles outside the small farming town where we lived. To my knowledge, the land wasn't owned by anyone in particular. There was a small, overgrown pathway just wide enough for a car that led back into the woods, perhaps the remnants of access to an old farmhouse that had once stood there. As we drove farther down the path and approached the woods, we came to a tiny wooden bridge that crossed a creek. It was barely wide enough for the car and there were no rails to keep us from going over the edge. Because I was a particularly anxious child who was easily overwhelmed by anything that I perceived as threatening, my happy-to-spend-the-day-outdoors attitude quickly turned into anxiety, despite the fact that the bridge wasn't high enough above the creek to place us in any danger.

Once across the bridge, my fear subsided and we continued down the path, drawing closer and closer to the woods. My grandfather pointed out a tree that had been struck by lightning, a deep, prominent scar winding its way down the trunk—a detail that only added to my already edgy state of mind. He parked his navy-blue station wagon, and we walked a short distance into the woods.

The wooded areas in the middle of farmland in Indiana are not as expansive as those in the southern part of the state. Most in northwest-central Indiana are small and patched randomly throughout the landscape. So it wasn't long before we came to a small clearing near the edge of the woods, with only a narrow line of trees separating them from a field. A noise from the field caused us both to stop. Suddenly, we spotted a deer just on the other side of the trees. It darted away as fast as its legs could carry it, with a few coyotes and a large dog in hot pursuit.

The deer and two of the coyotes continued on toward the darkening storm clouds off to the west, which were approaching at an alarming rate. But one of the coyotes and the dog turned and crossed the line of trees toward us. My grandfather, who walked with a cane due to a disability, told me to get behind him and held up his cane, preparing to fend off a possible attack. But the coyote and the dog just stood there staring at us—not with aggression or with fear, but with an alarmingly calm demeanor. They were perhaps fifteen to twenty feet away, certainly close enough to attack if they wanted to, but neither did. They just stood there quietly and stared. And as they did, I felt a sense of calm and protection wash over me. Then, as quickly as they had come, they were gone, running off through the field to catch up with their fellow predators and, hopefully, their prey.

Although the memory of that day has never left me, it wasn't until many years later that I really contemplated what that moment had meant to me—what connection had been made and why. It's possible that the calm and protection I felt resulted simply from my grandfather's presence and nothing more. But since then, I have come to see that moment as my first encounter with Anubis. Why the dog had joined the coyotes, I do not know. Maybe he ran away from a local farm to join them. Maybe it was just a random coincidence. But most domesticated dogs do not mix well with coyotes, so this one must have been roaming the wild for some time. Whatever the reason, the sense of calm and protection that I experienced that day were powerful feelings that I have only ever felt in the presence of the Obsidian Lord. So I can now appreciate that moment for what it was to me—Anubis seeking me out and giving me a little "hello" years prior to our working together formally. Little did I know then that we would connect about a decade later and establish a deep, personal, lifelong relationship.

The Beginning

From an early age, I was attuned to the spirits in the world around me. I frequently "saw" and "heard" spirits that others could not. I was raised by my grandparents, and my grandfather, although a self-proclaimed Christian, believed firmly in psychic abilities, reincarnation, spirits, and other phenomena with which many modern witches and Pagans align. It wasn't until I was older that I really embraced this, but I remember growing up unafraid of the unseen and unknown. I almost became more comfortable with them than I was with people.

It was on a summer night in 2001 that I started down the path to being a Pagan and a witch. In the house that I grew up in, I sometimes watched TV upstairs in the evening while my grandparents watched it in the living room. While randomly channel-surfing, I found a made-for-TV movie called *Mists of Avalon*. It told the story of King Arthur from the point of view of his sister Morgaine, who was a priestess of Avalon, a mysterious holy isle in Britain dedicated to the worship of the Mother Goddess. After watching the movie, I discovered it had been adapted from a book of the same title written by Marion Zimmer Bradley. Being a book lover and an avid reader, I immediately went and got a copy for myself and dove into it. It did not take me long to finish the book, despite it consisting of nearly 1,000 pages of complex plot and a multitude of characters.

After reading this highly controversial author, whose work I have since come to reject, I went on to discover other books, like Silver Ravenwolf's *Teen Witch* and Scott Cunningham's *Wicca: A Guide for the Solitary Practitioner* and its sequel *Living Wicca*. This in turn led me to a realization that there are many gods, goddesses, and spirits in the world around us, and that many of them are loving, caring entities. And that realization brought me comfort and solace. As a gay teen, I felt a sense of belonging and understanding that I had never felt in any other spiritual or religious path. It helped me find answers to questions I had been asking about the world around me and its mysteries. It helped me find the true beauty and deep spiritual meaning in the natural world, and it set me on the path to becoming a Pagan and a witch.

Within the first year of walking this path, I felt a calling to work with a specific deity. I knew there was a spirit out there somewhere who was waiting for me to reach out and make a connection. I did not know who it was at first, but I was okay with that, certain that, when the right time came, I would know. As I began to seek out information about the various pantheons of the world, I was first drawn to a particular archetype rather than a specific name, or even pantheon. Names like Hades, Pluto, the Morrigan, Hekate, Hel, Osiris, and Anubis jumped out at me, and I began seeing a theme of death and darkness, although I didn't know exactly why I was drawn to this theme. I understood the metaphorical meaning of death at that time, but I didn't really understand how it was relevant in my life, so I approached the theme of death quite literally. I had lost family members by that age, but had never been affected by it in ways that would cause me to reach out to a "god of death."

Despite that, I trusted my intuition, assuming there was something deeper there, perhaps something related to the transformative meaning of death. I became more and more attracted to the traditions and mythology of ancient Egypt, and eventually focused on Anubis. His energy felt extremely protective to me—full of strength, yet also compassionate. Although most reference books described him as being simply a god of embalming and funerary rights, this made no sense to me. I wasn't ready yet to think about a deity from thousands of years ago and connect it to the modern world. But I decided to investigate further and this led me to more and more information that confirmed that Anubis was much more complex than I had originally thought.

Nearly two and a half decades later, as I write this book, I now have a deep relationship with Anubis. There have been high points and low points in this relationship, and periods when one or both of us were silent. Life happens. And sometimes circumstances occurred that made me feel less connected to my spiritual path. Nevertheless, our relationship has grown and expanded in ways that I never imagined possible. And although I cannot claim to know all there is to know about Anubis—and with the caveat that it is impossible to know everything there is to know about *any* deity—I feel that I have enough experience to be able to share what I know about him with you.

In fact, I find that the many years during which Anubis has been a part of my spiritual life have left me with a great deal to say about him. I have come to know that he is more than just the Egyptian god of embalming and funerals, and he is more than just a jackal-headed god who lives in the shadows of a far-off desert. I have learned that he is a strong, protective force—one who cares for the souls of both the living and the dead. He protects the marginalized and those in pain. He stands for truth, justice, and integrity. He is supportive, yet also expects you to "do the work" and be self-sufficient and independent. He values authenticity, integrity, and honesty, yet is also understanding and compassionate.

Much of my relationship with Anubis is based on personal experience, mixed with the reading and research that I have done over the years. While I do not identify as a Kemetic Pagan—one who follows only the spiritual and religious practices of ancient Egypt, often from a reconstructionist point of view—I greatly admire those who do. Although I believe this can be an extremely fulfilling spiritual path for some, however, it is not mine. My approach to my relationship with Anubis—and any deity, for that matter—is gounded in my unique experiences in life and my own path as an independent practitioner.

Over the years, I have explored many practices from many spiritual paths, and even if I do not incorporate these into my own practice, I always find something of value in them. I align with multiple deities across multiple pantheons. I suppose you could say my practice is eclectic. I call myself a witch and a Pagan, but even those words are so broad that it is difficult to fully explain what they mean. My practice is uniquely informed by the things that I have read and done and experienced in life, and I believe that there is power in that. To me, *that* is what it means to be on a spiritual path. Each of us shapes our own path by the unique experiences we have in life. There is no such thing as cookie-cutter spirituality.

Ancient Gods in a Modern World

It is important to remember while reading this book that we live in a *modern* world, and we need to see deities through a modern lens. Many, or dare I say most, of those who follow any of the ancient Egyptian deities have no direct connection to the Egypt of old. I have no known Egyptian heritage, nor have I ever lived in Egypt, but that does not invalidate my practice or my experience. Our world is vastly different from the world of 2,000 or 3,000 years ago, and so it is not always relevant to try simply to recreate what was.

I cannot relate to Anubis as a god of mummification in a literal sense. In our modern society, we do not mummify our dead or our pets. Although embalming is still a modern practice, it looks quite different from the practices followed thousands of years ago. Nor do we bury our dead in elaborate tombs with their riches. But that does not mean that Anubis is irrelevant to us. There is absolutely a time and a place for continuing these ancient traditions and honoring their prayers, rituals, and practices. But there is also wisdom to be found in discovering how an ancient deity fits into our modern lives. Looking at these traditions and myths from a purely literal perspective is very limiting and misses the entire point of seeking a spiritual connection with a deity.

Myths can inform and inspire us, but we must be able to translate them into a context that makes them applicable today if they are to have any meaning for us. Myths can be incredibly interesting and they can serve as a foundational understanding of a deity, but we must not view them as "scripture" that must be closely followed. The most important thing about connecting with deities is the experiences *you* have with them. Not my experiences, or someone else's. Yours and yours alone.

Nor does your spiritual relationship with a deity have to align with how it has been viewed historically. I may connect coyotes with Anubis, even though they have not historically been associated with him—although there are species of coyotes found near Egypt. The truth is that your spiritual experiences and mine are *all* valid. Period.

How to Use This Book

My hope is that, in the pages that follow, you will come to understand a little more about Anubis. My goal is to provide you with information and to act as a guide to get you started building a relationship with him. Although some of what you will find here is based on the historical record, much of it is based on my own experiences. But my experiences with Anubis may not be the same as yours, and that's okay. In fact, that is one of the most beautiful things about deities. Each of us experiences them in different ways. There is no official manual or set of dogmatic rules that you must follow in building any spiritual relationship. Even if you are not a follower of Anubis, I hope this book piques your interest and curiosity.

This book consists of two parts. Part I contains information on who Anubis is, including his background and his myths, and an overview of the various roles he plays. Part II explores how to connect with Anubis and build a deeper relationship with him. As you read, particularly in Part I, it may help you to refer to Appendix A, which provides a brief historical timeline of ancient Egypt. The chapters are intended to be read in order, as they build on one another and give deeper insights as you move forward. But no matter whether you have worked with Anubis in the past or you are just starting out on your journey, there is something in this book for you. If you are just beginning your journey with Anubis, I welcome you. If you are experienced working with him, you may find that particular chapters interest you more than others.

Each chapter concludes with practices and journal prompts that are meant to encourage you to think more deeply about Anubis, the themes related to him, and your growing relationship with him. I strongly encourage you to keep a written record of your thoughts as you progress through the book. I recommend using a notebook dedicated to this practice, but if you already have a notebook that you have dedicated to spiritual exploration, like a Book of Shadows, then great! Use that. Write out any thoughts that are provoked by the journal prompts so that you have a record of your journey. Take notes as you go along on ideas, correspondences, passages, or names that stand out for you. This will help you along your path.

I hope that whoever you are and whatever your reason for reading this book, you can find something beneficial in its pages. Thank you for embarking on this journey with me.

Warmest blessings,
Charlie

Part One

DISCOVERING ANUBIS

Part One

DISCOVERING ANUBIS

CHAPTER 1

Who Is Anubis?

"The truth is harsh," Anubis said. "Spirits come to the Hall of Judgement all the time, and they cannot let go of their lies. They deny their faults, their true feelings, their mistakes . . . right up until Ammit devours their souls for eternity. It takes strength and courage to admit the truth."

RICK RIORDAN, *THE KANE CHRONICLES*

When you hear the name Anubis, what imagery does it conjure in your mind? Many people are familiar with the name, and perhaps even with the imagery of this popular god. When most think of ancient Egypt, they think of pyramids, deserts, and hieroglyphs. They may think of ancient wisdom shrouded in mystery and secrets buried deep in a far-off land of intense heat—a place where symbols of ancient knowledge are etched on the walls of tombs and temples, lost to time in the desert sands. This mysterious place and its traditions often feel distant and unfamiliar.

Many of the portrayals of ancient Egypt found in popular media include some kind of depiction of Anubis, either as a canid (dog-like) figure or a humanoid with the head of a canid. Even those who do not know him by name often immediately recognize him by his image. He can be found in pop culture in TV shows like *American Gods*—one of my favorite fictional representations of him that is based on the book by Neil Gaiman—and *Stargate,* as well as in movies like *Gods of Egypt, The Mummy*, and *The Mummy Returns.* His likeness appears in cartoons, video games, card games, and comic books.

Anubis is a many-faceted deity. He has been portrayed as a guide, a protector, and a guardian. He is variously known as Lord of Death, Master of Mysteries, Keeper of Keys, and Opener of Ways. He has been called Wise Elder, Master Healer, Chief Embalmer, and Upholder of Truth and Justice. He is recognized as a shaman, a bringer of balance, and a lord of liminal spaces. Of course, most modern portrayals of him are entirely fictional and are often grossly exaggerated fantastical depictions that are loosely based on who he is in reality. Nevertheless, he is recognized by many—even if only by his name and his association with death.

One of my favorite metaphysical stores near where I grew up in the Midwest had a five-foot statue of Anubis in the entrance to their library. He stood, ever watchful, facing the doorway, as if to both welcome visitors and protect the space. I always wished that statue had been for sale, because who doesn't need a life-sized statue of Anubis in their living room! But alas, he was merely there to guide the inquisitive and protect the historical and occult knowledge that lay within.

Meet Anubis

Anubis is one of the oldest gods in the Egyptian pantheon, so ancient that evidence indicates that he may predate many other Egyptian deities. Thus his origins are difficult to pinpoint. Depictions of him in full form date as far back as 3100 BCE, possibly earlier. Moreover, the association between jackals and death dates back even farther than that, perhaps as far back as 6000 BCE. Worship of Anubis predates the worship of Osiris as Lord of Death, as well as the rise in popularity of Osiris and his siblings, Isis, Nephthys, and Set.

To the best of our knowledge, Anubis was originally worshipped as the god of the dead and the Underworld, and at a significantly earlier date than many other Egyptian gods of the dead. He is sometimes described as the son of Ra, god of the sun, and Hesat, a goddess depicted as the cow that gifted milk to humanity and who is sometimes considered to be an aspect of the great goddess Hathor, mother goddess and goddess of love, fertility, and beauty.

In the tales written by Greek philosopher and historian Plutarch, Anubis is described as a son of Nephthys and Osiris who was raised by Osiris and Isis. We'll revisit this myth in greater detail in chapter 2. Some alternative myths claim he is the son of Set and Nephthys. Others connect him to the sun, to the earth, to life, and to death, to name just a few of his associations. These conflicting origin stories give some insight into how incredibly complex and influential a deity he is.

Most place Anubis's origins in Cynopolis, ancient Greek for "City of Dogs," which is now the modern-day city of Al Qays. Wepwawet, another canid-headed deity, was later associated with Anubis. Wepwawet, usually identified as a wolf, originated in a city then called Lycopolis, ancient Greek for "City of Wolves," today known as Asyut. As I will discuss in later chapters, Anubis and Wepwawet were closely connected and were often depicted opposite one another.

Anubis held dominion over elaborate funerary grounds known as *necropoli,* "cities of the dead," in places like Saqqara, where eight million mummified dogs have been found buried. It's thought that these were not the result of sacrifices, but rather offerings of deceased pets that were given to Anubis so that he would protect them in the afterlife. Animals and their spiritual significance were incredibly important in ancient Egypt, as we can see from the fact that the gods were connected to animals, and that animals were often mummified and buried in the same way that kings and queens were—sometimes even alongside them.

The myths surrounding Osiris, initially the royal god of agriculture and civilization who later became god of the Underworld, and Isis, goddess of healing and magick, changed the way Egyptians worshipped Anubis. When Osiris took on his more popular aspects as god of the Underworld and of rebirth, Anubis's role, in turn, shifted to that of god of mummification and embalming. When this happened, his origin story shifted as well, his parents being identified as either Osiris and Nephthys, a river goddess later associated with death and mourning, or Nephthys and Set, god of chaos and storms. Although this may seem like a "demotion," so to speak, his role and importance were still vitally important, as we all know that mummification and embalming were an important part of funerary rites at that time.

In his new role, Anubis was petitioned to watch over and guide the souls of the dead on their journey from the physical realm to the afterlife. Osiris took on the rather passive role of a figurehead, while Anubis did all of the work of guiding the dead, protecting them, and presiding over the judgment of their souls. In a sense, Osiris became like the boss who makes his subordinates do all the work while he sits in his office and takes all the credit.

After this shift occurred, Anubis's role in the afterlife—the one with which we are most familiar today—became more prominent and more popular. In addition to his role as protector and usher of souls, he presided over the Hall of Judgment (also known as the Hall of Two Truths), where souls went upon death to be judged. This ceremony, known as the Weighing of the Heart, involved the deceased's heart being weighed against the Feather of Ma'at, which represented order, balance, truth, integrity, and justice in the universe. Sometimes this was also depicted in goddess form, as a woman with outstretched wings wearing a white ostrich feather on her head.

The souls who were deemed "unbalanced" were fed to Ammit the Devourer, a demon with the front of a lion, the back of a hippo, and the head of a crocodile. This horrible creature, who was at the beck and call of Anubis, consumed the souls of those found wanting. While Osiris oversaw this whole process, it was Anubis who actually performed the ceremony. This is why you often see him either holding a set of scales or standing near them (see chapter 6).

Worship and Influence

In the thousands of years that have passed since the period we now call ancient Egypt, Anubis has played multiple roles and was perceived from various angles. As Great Guardian, his fierce likeness was placed in tombs to protect those laid to rest there by punishing any who disrespected or desecrated the space. His statues were placed facing outward at the entrance of the tombs to guard the bodies of the deceased from any who dared enter. His image and his name were carved onto the western walls of tombs—a direction associated with death in ancient Egypt—facing the mummified bodies to protect them.

Anubis was usually revered as a protective, caring deity, but this was not always the case. Over time, particularly during the later eras when Greeks and Romans invaded and conquered Egypt (see Appendix A), he became feared and his name was invoked to spark terror in the hearts of enemies. Curses invoked the wrath of Anubis against anyone who dared enter a tomb with malign intent. In fact, two of his epithets—Dog Who Swallows Millions and One Who Eats His Father—refer to the jackals and wild dogs of the desert who were known to dig up shallow graves and consume the remains of the dead buried there.

Apart from being protector of the dead, Anubis had other important roles related to death as well. He was invoked during the embalming process, and was said to have invented the art of embalming and mummification in order to revive the dead god Osiris (see chapter 2). Priests called on him during the embalming and mummification processes. He was a guide in the afterlife, leading the deceased to their final destination, and presided over the Weighing of the Heart ceremony to determine a soul's worthiness to enter the afterlife.

In 305 BCE, the Ptolemaic Kingdom of Egypt was founded by Ptolemy I Soter, a companion of Alexander the Great. As the Greeks settled in Egypt, they developed their own Hellenistic interpretation of Anubis, blending him with their own god Hermes (see chapter 9). Both deities served as "psychopomps"—spiritual escorts to the realm of the dead. This blended deity was known as Hermanubis, although in chapter 9 we'll examine how this may be a misinterpretation of a blended Horus and Anubis. Because of this blending, people eventually began to view Anubis as a cult symbol, invoking him in magick and spell work alongside other deities like Hekate.

Later, during the Roman occupation of Egypt, Anubis developed a bit of a dark cult following, with necromancers invoking him as Keeper of Keys to the Underworld. In this role, he brought forth the spirits of the deceased from the land of the dead so that they could be questioned. Thus he became associated with curses and hexes. With the advent of Christianity, these necromantic cult practices were shunned as evil. Today, Anubis is often portrayed cinematically as a powerful god who leads an army of demons who curse those who cross him.

The Dog-Headed God

The Egyptian pantheon contains multiple canid deities, although Anubis was arguably one of the most widely known and worshipped. In fact, his popularity spread rapidly into Europe and he has survived into the modern era. Depictions of him have been found in tombs and temples throughout Egypt, where he was often depicted as a black canid—most commonly interpreted as a jackal—sitting upon a pedestal, an altar, or a platform of some kind.

It's hard to know exactly what kind of canid Anubis is, however. The jackals found in Egypt aren't black, so why is he so often identified as a jackal? In the hot, unforgiving desert sands, death was cruel. Only a few animals could survive in that environment, one of which was the jackal. Although they sometimes hunted small animals, jackals were mostly scavengers, relying on carrion for food in order to conserve their energy in the intense heat. They dug up shallow graves and ate the remains of the dead. Thus it makes sense that, in the more primitive culture of pre-dynastic Egypt before the time of the kings and pharaohs, people prayed to animals native to the desert—including jackals—for protection and guidance and to ensure that the remains of their dead were not eaten.

Anubis the jackal.

Some modern Egyptologists note that the canid form of Anubis could also be that of a wild or domesticated dog, a fox, or even a now-extinct species of jackal more closely related to wolves and coyotes. All of these were found in predynastic Egypt. The difficulty in clarifying this is that artistic representations in ancient Egypt were not realistic and relied on the use of symbolism. So it's impossible to know exactly what was intended in these portrayals. One possible explanation is that these depictions represent an archetype that encompasses multiple canids that all have similar appearances, similar behaviors, and similar symbolic meanings.

Anubis was also commonly portrayed as a figure with the body of a man and the head of a black canid. Rarely was he ever depicted in full human form, although there are a few instances of this. As with many Egyptian deities, he was often shown with an ankh or a staff, which symbolized the cycles of life, death, and rebirth. Pharaohs were often buried with small statues of Anubis in hopes that he would not only protect their bodies, but help guide them in the afterlife.

Statue of Anubis depicting him in human form with the head of a black canid.

One of the best-known depictions of Anubis was found in the now-famous tomb of Tutankhamun, a boy king who was thought to be disabled and died at a young age. The tomb of King Tut, as he came to be known in the modern world, is a rare instance of a tomb that was found entirely intact and undisturbed. Discovered in 1922 by an archaeological team led by famous British archaeologist and Egyptologist Howard Carter, this tomb contained a large statue of Anubis, portrayed as a dog-like figure seated atop a pedestal directly inside the doorway to the tomb, facing outward to guard the entrance. A little-known fact is that, upon its discovery, the statue of Anubis was adorned with layers of shrouds, a sash, and a garland of flowers. These were later removed as the treasures of the tomb were retrieved, and now the statue is displayed without them in a museum in Cairo. The sash, similar to those worn around the waists of pharaohs, gods, and goddesses, was a symbol of protection and of those who protect, representationally thought to come from the hieroglyph for the word for "amulet."

Shrouded Anubis, guarding the entrance to King Tut's Tomb.

What's in a Name?

Anubis has many names, titles, and epithets. In fact, it's hard to know today exactly how his name was pronounced, as we are thousands of years removed from the language of ancient Egypt. This is now classified as a "dead" language—one that, like Sanskrit, no longer has either native or secondary speakers and that now exists thanks only to the efforts of archaeologists and linguists. Thanks to these scholars, we have now been able to reconstruct our understanding of this ancient language and what it may have sounded like.

The language of ancient Egypt was written in a variety of ways, including using the hieroglyphics we associate with it today. Hieroglyphs are symbols or signs that represent a particular sound, although certain vowel sounds were not written at all. Thus we can hypothesize that Anubis's Egyptian name would have been something similar to *Anpu*, or *Inpw*, based on the sounds associated with the hieroglyphs used to write it (see page 20). Although these symbols are difficult to interpret exactly, it's thought that the name may possibly mean "royal child," "prince," "puppy," or even "decay." When the Greeks came into Egypt, they called him Ἄνουβις, from which we get the name Anubis, the name by which he is most commonly known today. Many who work with him closely, however, prefer to call him by his Egyptian name. Personally, I switch between the two somewhat arbitrarily, although I tend to call him Anpu when I wish to be more formal.

Perhaps the most famous hieroglyph associated with ancient Egypt and its spirituality is the *ankh,* a symbol that represented the word for "life" or "breath of life." It looks sort of like a cross with a loop at the top, although it is thousands of years older than the cross used in Christianity. The ankh represented the cycles of life, immortality, rebirth, and the afterlife. It also became a protective symbol worn by both ancient and modern practitioners. Gods and goddesses were frequently depicted with an ankh to represent their divinity. Although its origins are uncertain, it is thought perhaps to be derived from the intersection of water, air, earth, and the sun—the in-between spaces that provide the foundations of life.

Hieroglyph that represents the name Anubis.

We learned to decipher the meaning of hieroglyphics thanks to the discovery of the Rosetta Stone, a famous tablet found in 1799 in the deserts of Egypt by Pierre-François Bouchard, an officer in the French Army of Engineers. I had the chance to see this remarkable artifact, which is now located in the British Museum, during a trip I made to the U.K. in my middle school years. The stone contains a text written in three ancient languages extant around the time of its creation (circa 196 BCE)—hieroglyphics, ancient Greek, and Demotic, an ancient Egyptian language derived from hieratic, the shorthand written form of hieroglyphics. Demotic was the precursor of the Coptic language that is still used by Coptic Christians today in religious ceremonies, in the same way that Latin is used in the Roman Catholic church. It is spoken in religious ceremonies and rituals, but rarely in the wider world.

Our understanding of ancient Greek, which evolved into what we know as modern Greek, had been well established by the time of the discovery of the Rosetta Stone, as there were countless texts that had been translated into Latin and other languages. This, combined with the knowledge of Coptic, enabled linguists and archaeologists to decipher the meaning of the hieroglyphs on the stone. Indeed, the discovery of the Rosetta Stone is the primary reason we have been able to piece together the meaning of the ancient hieroglyphic system and how names may have been pronounced. Still, despite this linguistic success, it is impossible to know the exact meanings or pronunciation of the words. Experts can only make educated estimates based on the knowledge gained by deciphering the stone.

Epithets

Epithets are names or titles given to deities by their worshippers to represent aspects of their power. They are commonly used among modern Pagans and witches who wish to connect with a particular aspect of a deity, but they aren't a new phenomenon. They were widely used in the ancient world, and most of them are very old and must be discovered through the study of ancient texts. Epithets were commonly used to refer to deities in the Egyptian and Greek pantheons and certainly existed in other pantheons, although perhaps less conspicuously.

The choice of using a particular epithet is a personal one. Many who follow specific deities choose not to use them at all, addressing them by their most commonly known name. However, should you choose to use epithets, they can help you to connect to certain aspects of deities and deepen your relationship with them. Of course, you can do this without the use of epithets as well. The choice is up to you.

I have only been using epithets for the last few years to connect with deities, including Anubis. And I feel that it has made a difference in my practice. I think that it has brought me closer to the deities that I follow by focusing on specific energies that they bring. It also seems to help me understand them on a deeper level.

Deciphering epithets of Egyptian gods and goddesses comes with challenges, however, not the least of which is that many of the writings that once existed have long been forgotten or lost over time. Who knows what secrets are buried in the sands of Egypt and surrounding areas? And who knows what has been lost forever due to natural disasters, natural decay, thievery, and human destruction?

Moreover, hieroglyphics can be incredibly challenging to interpret, so it becomes a matter of relying on those few who can read them and understand them. Years of studying hieroglyphics and their meaning can still leave you baffled as to what they actually represent, and you are left with little choice except to rely on those who are skilled in translating them. Add to this the possibility of human error, personal interpretations, and bias, and you have some idea of how challenging epithets can be.

In addition, it's sometimes hard to fully comprehend the intended meaning of a particular epithet, simply because the everyday use of it is thousands of years removed from our modern Pagan, Kemetic, and witch practices, as well as from academic contexts. Thus it's important to take into consideration the historical, cultural, geographical, religious, and environmental factors that may have contributed to the use and meaning of an epithet—at least as much as we are able. The Internet can provide some information, but generally not its original source. And even if you can find source information, reading and understanding it can be a bit of a chore in itself. The descriptions of epithets used in this book are not always literal translations, but rather translations of meaning and intention as I've interpreted them in my own practice.

Anubis is referred to by many epithets that point to his various aspects—as god of the dead, guide in the afterlife, protector of souls, healer, holder of secrets, and more. The fact that he has both Egyptian and Greek epithets indicates that his influence was felt beyond the sands of Egypt. You will find both in this book, and we'll look at their meaning and usage through the lens of a modern practitioner of witchcraft and/or Paganism. Please note that I am a rather eclectic Pagan, meaning that I incorporate some of my own spiritual thoughts and understandings into my practice. These, while based on historical information, are grounded in my own experiences and interpretations.

There are many more epithets of Anubis than will be mentioned in the chapters that follow, and many of these are hard to find in ancient texts. The ones I include here are just a small sampling of some of the more common ones.

Learning to pronounce epithets can be a challenge as well, especially since we only have linguists' and Egyptologists' understanding of the language to rely on for guidance. That being said, use whatever form of the epithets you're most comfortable with—the Egyptian version or the English translation. It's the intention behind the practice that matters most. Use epithets in prayers, invocations, and meditations. Speak them to connect to a particular aspect of Anubis. Etch them into candles in spells or draw symbolic representations of them to use as sigils. There are many ways you can integrate them into your practice, and we'll examine some of them in the chapters to come.

History vs. Modernism

Fully understanding who Anubis is from a historical perspective is challenging, if not impossible. The thing about looking back at what we consider to be "ancient Egypt" is that it spanned thousands of years. The pyramids were already thousands of years old by the time Cleopatra lived. Think about how much would have changed in that amount of time, let alone between then and today. Empires grew and fell. Pharaohs lived and died. Populations moved. Beautiful temples were built in dedication to gods and goddesses, only to be abandoned later and buried in the sands of time. Tombs were raided and emptied.

The King Haremhab with Anubis.

The worship of all deities changed drastically over the course of time. Because of this, from our perspective today, we are often confronted with contradictions and conclusions that don't appear to make sense at first glance. As societies changed and evolved over the millennia that separate us from ancient Egypt, the worship of gods was essentially left to the interpretation of those who followed them, often priests and pharaohs. This means that the same deities may have been worshipped in different ways in various places at various times. This makes it nearly impossible to trace information on a god to one single source or even one time period. The gods changed even within what we now call "ancient Egypt," and they have certainly changed since then. The beauty of that, however, is that we, as modern practitioners and worshippers, can play a part in discovering who they were and defining how they fit into our modern world. Our own interpretations of the gods and goddesses of the world continue to shape how they are seen today.

Today, we have the opportunity to see the gods through the lens of sophisticated technology and complex sociological, economic, and political phenomena. And it makes sense to do this. We do not live in the world of 3,000 years ago, so it doesn't make sense to base our understanding of them entirely on that. Humanity has changed, and so have the gods. The Hellenistic goddess Athena, for example, is known as a goddess of battle and wisdom, but not everyone can relate to that. Taking a broader view, you can see that she is not just a goddess of literal battle and war, but can be helpful when fighting a battle for justice. There are no longer many blacksmiths out there, but the Celtic goddess Brigid can still be petitioned for many creative endeavors.

This is why gods of death like Anubis, Hekate, the Morrigan, Hel, Hades, and Osiris will always be relevant. Chthonic and death gods are always around, because death is a constant. These "dark" deities are not "evil" at all, but rather powerful forces associated with death, the Underworld/Otherworld realms, and the harder aspects of life. Thus they are more relevant than ever. We live in a challenging world that seems to be getting more challenging and more complex each year. In these times of change and chaos, a god or goddess standing at your side and leading you through the darkness can be a powerful ally.

Anubis is not just a god who was worshipped in a far-off land more than 4,000 years ago. He is not someone reachable only by learning hieroglyphics and memorizing ancient spells. Although you can certainly do that, it is not the only way to approach him. Anubis's influence spread across Egypt and into Europe, and the Greeks and Romans continued to worship him even after the decline of Egyptian culture. Today he enjoys a cult-like following of practitioners who petition him for magick, spells, divination, and communing with the dead. *This* is why you find him today in metaphysical stores, in libraries, and on the Internet. His influence has never died. He still lives, resting in the shadows and dark corners of our world, bringing them into the light so that they may be transformed.

Gratitude Prayer to Anubis

Hail Anubis, Lord of Death!
Sovereign of the Underworld,
Protector and Guardian,
Guide and Healer,
Shaman and Wise Elder,
He Who Walks Between Worlds.
I offer my thanks for your wisdom and guidance,
For your presence and your protection,
For teaching me the mysteries.
May I walk between worlds, as you do,
Seeing the magick and mystery in the world
And honoring the deceased and those who have come before.
Dua Anpu!

Journal Prompts

- What do you already know about Anubis?
- Where have you encountered him or his likeness before?
- What more do you wish to learn about Anubis?

CHAPTER 2

Mythological Origins

Myth is the secret opening through which the inexhaustible energies of the cosmos pour into human manifestation.

JOSEPH CAMPBELL

Myths can be extremely informative and can function as a foundation for understanding the nature and power of the gods and goddesses they portray. There are so many wonderful myths that come from the tombs, temple walls, and scrolls of ancient Egypt, however, that it can be overwhelming. In fact, there is more to read and digest than seems humanly possible. And this means that, as you begin to examine this rich and ancient resource, you will almost certainly encounter things that may seem a bit contradictory.

These contradictions are abundantly clear in the origin myths of Anubis. Plutarch wrote that Anubis was the offspring of Osiris and Nephthys, although he was raised by Osiris and Isis. But a little research turns up writings that claim he is much, much older than many of these other deities. In these sources, he is referred to as the son of Ra and Hesat, or even Ra and Bast, feline goddess of perfumes, dance, and passion, and a protectress of Ra. Despite being contradictory, however, these stories can be quite informative, because they give you a picture of the lives of the worshippers of that time. They reveal how the gods were perceived and how they were honored, and even tell you a little about their personalities and how you can interact with them.

This, of course, does not mean that our understanding of gods and goddesses is limited to what we find in history and myths. Modern interpretations and experiences can be just as relevant, if not more so. My experiences—and yours—are just as valid, and we need not be limited to the information unearthed in tombs and scrawled on temple walls thousands of years ago. Are there aspects of these deities that modern followers experience that perhaps didn't exist thousands of years ago? Yes, absolutely. Times change, people change, and our interpretations of the gods change as well.

So as you read these myths, think about them, but take them with a grain of salt. Remember: Myths are, by definition, not facts.

Birth of a God

The best-known origin story of Anubis—although not one without contradiction—appears in Plutarch's *Moralia* (circa 100 CE), which tells the story of Osiris, Isis, Nephthys, and Set, the four children of Nut, goddess of the night sky, and Geb, god of the earth. Osiris originally had dominion over civilization and agriculture and was seen as a benevolent god who blessed his followers and helped their crops grow. His brother Set was a trickster god of chaos, the desert, and storms—a jealous, angry, and vengeful god who was also known as a warrior and protector. His sister Isis was a goddess of magick, light, and healing, while Nephthys, her darker twin, was a goddess of magick and death, and especially of mourning and grief. She was also associated with rivers.

Osiris and Isis, who were partnered early on, had a child named Horus, the bright god of light and the skies who became heir to the throne. Set, associated with the infertile desert sands, was partnered by default with Nephthys. When they were unable to conceive a child, Nephthys decided to play a trick on Osiris by disguising herself as her twin, Isis, and seducing him. The child born of this union was Anubis, the princely god of death. Knowing that Set would be angry and seek to kill the child, Nephthys hid him in the desert, where he was found by Isis and her dogs. Isis took him to be raised by herself and Osiris, and Anubis became her protector and guardian.

This myth only adds to the confusion surrounding Anubis's origins. As we saw in the last chapter, several sources claim that he may have been the son of Ra and Hesat, or of Ra and Bast. Now we have a story claiming that he may be the son of Osiris and Nephthys, which makes Isis his stepmother and Set his stepfather. Some sources even claim that he is actually the son of Set and Nephthys. All of this is almost certain to leave you confused and frustrated, asking questions to which there are no answers.

But I personally think that these conflicting stories serve rather to demonstrate that Anubis is an incredibly complex deity who just doesn't fit into one neat little box. He is a god whose reach spans time and space, myth and mystery. If anything, these contradictions demonstrate his importance. Either he is the son of one king of the gods (Ra) or another (Osiris). Either way, he is a royal child, which is one interpretation of the name Anpu. These conflicting myths also highlight his connection to various aspects of the universe, encompassing life and death, and light and darkness.

In fact, this myth really demonstrates how worshippers in ancient Egypt shifted their views on Osiris and Anubis, and how many came to associate Osiris with death and the Underworld. When Osiris fathered a son with Nephthys, Set, who had always resented his brother's status and popularity, became angry. In a fit of rage, he killed Osiris, chopped his body into pieces, and scattered them across Egypt. Yikes!

But Isis, Osiris's beloved wife, gathered together as many of the gods as she could to help her find the pieces of his body. With Anubis acting as guardian and protector, they found all the pieces except his penis. And this is when Anubis invented embalming and mummification. With his help, Isis crafted the missing penis out of clay and put her husband back together. Then she petitioned Thoth to teach her the magick needed to revive Osiris and brought him back to life. Easy enough for a goddess, right?

In another version of the myth, Horus battles Set seeking revenge for his father's death, and Anubis later kills Set for trying to steal Osiris's body during the process of mummification. Whichever of these versions you choose to accept, it is through this act of death and rebirth that Osiris comes to oversee the Underworld

Here we see Anubis fulfilling many of his classical roles—protector, guardian, embalmer, and god of death. From this point on, however, Osiris also becomes associated with death, while Anubis's role shifts primarily to embalming and mummification. This is when Anubis becomes a psychopomp and weigher of hearts. As we have seen, although Osiris is called King of the Underworld and Lord of Judgment, it is Anubis who plays the *active* role in death. He is the one whom most petitioned for guidance and protection in the afterlife. Although some of his epithets may have changed, his power and influence never did.

The Battle of Anubis and Set

During the lengthy process of embalming and mummification, Set plotted to steal Osiris's body and destroy it, knowing that, until he was completely destroyed, he wasn't *fully* gone. Disguising himself as Anubis, he snuck into the embalming temple and stole his brother's body.

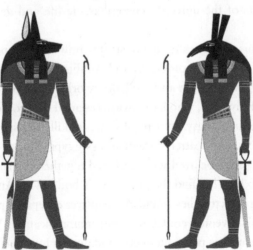

Anubis (left) and Set (right).

It wasn't long before Anubis discovered this (he is known as the Great Watcher, after all!) and pursued Set. Set attempted to thwart Anubis by turning himself into a bull, only to have Anubis castrate him and imprison him in the desert. Set escaped, this time turning himself into a leopard. Anubis caught him again and branded him with a hot iron—thus giving the leopard its spots. After several more attemps, Anubis had finally had enough. He flayed Set and burned his body. Then he entered Set's camp cloaked in his skin and murdered his entire army with one blow. And that is why this region of Egypt has ever since had reddish soil and rocks.

You can see here that Anubis doesn't put up with those with evil intent. He keeps a watchful eye out for those who wish to harm the dead whom he protects. And protect them he will, at any cost. Although he can be kind and caring, he doesn't put up with malign actions.

As you can see, myths can be incredibly interesting, even in their apparent contradictions. They tell unique tales of the gods and portray them in a light that allows us to see who they were and how they lived their lives. They aren't meant to be factual, however. Rather, they serve to inform us and give us insight. Keep that in mind as you work with Anubis. You may discover that there are things about him that are different from, or even contradict, what is portrayed above. Remember that these myths, although perhaps *inspired* by the gods, were ultimately transcribed by humans who had their own thoughts and opinions on a variety of subjects.

Prayer for Wisdom

Hail the Master of Secrets!
Anubis, the Keeper of Keys,
I stand at the doors to the Great Mysteries.
Show me the path that will help me the most.
Help me to discover the knowledge and wisdom I need.
Show me my key.

Journal Prompts

- What myths about Anubis do you find most interesting?

- How do you interpret the myths given in this chapter?

- How do you feel that these myths are relevant to a modern spiritual practice, if at all?

CHAPTER 3

Lord of Death and Transformation

Anubis shows me a large, oblong cocoon hanging from a great tree. "What is it?" I ask. He tells me to be patient and that all will be revealed and understood. Slightly impatiently, I wait to see what is going to happen. I begin to wonder, and my curiosity grows.

Before long, the shell begins to crack. Slowly, more and more pieces of it begin to fall away. I can see something stirring inside. Then wings begin to emerge. They are beautiful shades of green, blue, aqua, purple, and turquoise, and every shade in between. They are quite beautiful. I begin to tear up, but I cannot explain why. Then something unexpected emerges that shocks me.

Me. I am the one with wings. I am the one in the cocoon. I am transformed.

ANUBIS TO ME IN A VISION

had this vision during a time of great change in my life. At the time, it was shocking, but it will stay forever in my memory as a reminder that change is not necessarily bad. Although it can be incredibly uncomfortable, even painful, sometimes change is exactly what is needed in order for something new and beautiful to emerge. Anubis is the Lord of Death, the ultimate transformation in life. He stands there, waiting and watching as the transformation in your life takes place, and he can be petitioned for guidance and protection during these times.

Death can be viewed from several perspectives—some literal, some symbolic; some positive, some negative; some light, some dark; some signifying endings, some signifying beginnings. In this chapter, we will explore one of the deeper meanings of death—the idea of death as a process, a process that includes transformation, growth, and rebirth.

The Dark Side of Death

It's hard to deny that death has a dark side. There are ugly truths that stare you in the face. Death can be brutal, cruel, and unforgiving. It can come about through murder, disease, poison, pestilence, suffering, horrific accidents, and myriad other disturbing causes. Death is the cold embrace of the night in forever's winter. Death is decay and decomposition. It induces fear. In nature, vultures, jackals, corvids, and many other creatures feast on the remains of the dead. Although many are frightened or disturbed by these creatures, in fact they function as nature's "clean-up crew." Vultures, for example, have incredibly strong stomachs that can break down all of the bacteria and even diseases that most other animals could not stomach (literally).

This is likely why many deities associated with death are perceived as harsh and punishing. When someone you love dies, it may feel as if that person is being taken from you as a punishment for something you've done. And who knows for sure what lies beyond death? Some cultures threaten you with the possibility of going to a horrendous place of suffering if you don't "live right." Some seek to appease gods of death so that, when they die, they may find some relief from the pain and torment of what may come next. It's the uncertainty—the unknown—that can be terrifying to think about.

I remember the first dead person I saw. My great-grandfather passed away when I was six years old. I do not remember all of the details, but I distinctly remember seeing his body lying in the casket and touching his cold, stiff hand. I was not afraid. I understood that he was no longer with us—that he had moved on. I hadn't been forced into a situation that I was not ready for. It was just an interesting event for me. Since then, I have lost several important figures in my life—great-grandparents, a best friend, classmates, and even my beloved grandfather. I was with my grandfather when he passed. I remember every single detail of the moments that led up to his death and the last moments of his life. That experience is something that will remain with me for the rest of my life.

Losing a loved one is never easy. It sticks with you. It changes you. It is full of grief, sorrow, and ugly crying. But I have also come to see death as a beautiful transformation from one phase to the next. Understanding what comes next, if you have any belief in that sort of thing, can be a comforting thought, especially if your loved one was suffering from physical or mental ailments in this life. Getting to that point of understanding, however, can take a very long time—months and even years—and even then, parts of that grief can persist. But eventually, the pain will ease little by little.

Because of this dark side, death has somehow become a forbidden topic in our American culture. We simply do not talk about it. We, as a society, are terrified of death—of the cold, harsh, and unforgiving nature of it. Death has become an uncomfortable topic that is always associated with feelings we do not want to face, including grief, heartache, and sorrow.

But while grieving is a natural part of dealing with death, death can also be a celebration of life. In fact, today, an interesting shift in our views on death appears to be taking place. Celebrations of life are happening more and more often in modern families who want to remember their loved ones in a positive light. These celebrations are not meant to diminish grief or attempt to stuff it away entirely; instead, they are meant to honor the memory of loved ones, acknowledge that they have moved on to something better, and celebrate them as the people they were (see chapter 16).

This is not, by any means, a new practice, however. Cultures around the world have been doing this for hundreds, if not thousands, of years. Some cultures in Central America celebrate the *Día de los Muertos* (Day of the Dead), a holiday dedicated to honoring and celebrating their ancestors and loved ones who have passed on. On this day, they visit their graves and adorn them with beautiful flowers. Families build altars dedicated to the deceased and decorate them with photos, mementos, and even favorite foods that remind them of their loved ones. They leave a special place at meals for family members who have moved on. They light candles and say prayers to invite the spirits of departed loved ones to bless the family. These practices all acknowledge the grief and loss of death, but they also take time to celebrate the dead.

In East Asian spiritual traditions, ancestral veneration is an important component of daily life. Family members dedicate shrines to their ancestors, leaving offerings, burning incense, and praying to them for guidance. They place great emphasis on living a life that will make their ancestors proud.

Death Rituals in Ancient Egypt

We tend to associate ancient Egypt strongly with death. This may have to do with what we can immediately see. The ancient remains of everyday buildings like homes have long since returned to the earth, and the ruins that we do still have are those of important buildings like temples and tombs that were built out of durable, long-lasting materials like stone. In fact, most of the structures that have survived from ancient Egypt are places that were associated with death. And from what they tell us, death was clearly a very important part of life in this culture.

In the Old Kingdom, from roughly 2700 BCE to roughly 2200 BCE, only the kings (pharaohs) were guaranteed passage into the afterlife, and it required riches and wealth to be granted that passage. Kings were seen as extensions of the divine, and they were granted special privileges in both this life and the afterlife. Servants of kings and those who embalmed them upon death might earn passage to the afterlife through merit, but most others could not. By the Middle Kingdom, however, everyone had a chance at the afterlife, provided they lived their lives in as well-intentioned a way as possible.

Ancient Egyptians mummified their dead in order to preserve their remains so that, after death, the soul could return to the body and reanimate it. This is why the dead were buried with shrouds and death masks—to make it easier for souls to find their bodies again. They defined the soul as having three equally important parts—the *ka*, the *ba*, and the *akh*.

The ka was the part of the spirit that looked like a person. It was, in a sense, made in a person's image. It was the part of the soul that needed sustenance in the afterlife, just as in life. The ba was the part of the soul that represented who a person was on the inside—their likes and dislikes, their personality, their desires, and their important characteristics. The akh was the union of the two, the complete person who lived in the after-life that comprised all of who they had been in this life.

We'll talk more about these beliefs and rituals in chapter 4. Suffice it to say here that these death rituals were seen as a means by which to ensure that those lucky enough to undergo them enjoyed happy, peaceful, and prosperous afterlives.

In ancient Egypt, Anubis was the original god of death, long before Osiris's death and his ascension to the role of god of the Underworld. Even long after, however, Anubis was present throughout Egyptian cul-ture as a reminder of the significance of death and as a protector. He played a role throughout the entire process of death. Many prayed to him on their deathbeds. He participated in the embalming process, overseeing the difficult work that the embalmers, priests, and funerary workers per-formed. Followers of the ancient traditions prayed to him for guidance and protection throughout their lives and as they transitioned into the afterlife. He was just as much a guardian of the living as of the dead.

Images and statues of Anubis were placed into the tombs of kings and pharaohs, and even those of common folk, for protection and guid-ance. He guided souls of the deceased through the Underworld—known as the *Duat*—to the Hall of Judgment, where he oversaw the Weighing of the Heart ceremony to determine the deceased's fate. From there, he guided them to the Field of Reeds, where he protected them and guarded them. He helped the living commune with the dead, and helped lost souls find their way. His role in death was broad and expansive.

Khenti-Amentiu

But Anubis was not the only Egyptian deity associated with death. As we have seen, Osiris also played an important role in the Underworld, as did another deity named Khenti-Amentiu, whose name means Foremost of the Westerners. It is widely accepted among Egyptologists, scholars, and the majority of Kemetic practitioners that Khenti-Amentiu was originally a separate deity from both Anubis and Osiris. Later, however, his name became associated with Anubis, perhaps as an aspect of him, and a loose connection was established between the two deities. It is also possible that the name Khenti-Amentiu was used as a title for Anubis and may have been used to refer to Osiris as well. Today, the name is widely used as an epithet associated with Anubis, primarily because its meaning is tied closely to death.

Osiris-Khenti-Amentiu and Anubis

Khenti-Amentiu was associated with the necropolis, particularly at Abydos. He was often portrayed as a mummified man wearing the crown of Egypt. Other depictions show him as a jackal-headed humanoid, similar to Anubis. His worship originated in Abydos, but as Osiris's popularity grew, Khenti-Amentiu seemed to fade in importance and eventually merged with Osiris and Anubis. Anubis continued to be worshipped at Abydos in the same role as Khenti-Amentiu.

The name Foremost of the Westerners may sound a bit odd (perhaps due to the translation), but it can convey a number of meanings. It may refer to the dead themselves, since Egyptians believed that the sun died in the west each day and was reborn in the east. This association with death may be the intended meaning of the term "Westerners"—referring to those whose time on earth had passed—and the title was thus reserved for the god of the dead. Another possible interpretation lies in the fact that the entrance to the Underworld was thought to lie in the west—again, perhaps because the west was associated with the dead. The deceased had to pass through the west, as did the sun, to enter the land of the dead.

In light of this, it makes sense to call Anubis Khenti-Amentiu, or Lord of Death, because his associations with death were so important, and there were many necropoli and catacombs dedicated to him. His likeness was carved onto the walls of many tombs and painted upon countless coffins. Statues of him were placed in the tombs along with the deceased because he was their staunch guardian and defender. His image served to protect them from any person or entity who wished to harm them. He also served as a guide to ensure that, upon reawakening, the deceased could find their way to a happy, peaceful afterlife.

Death as Transformation

Let's stop here for a moment to ponder what exactly death means metaphorically. Everyone dies, right? Yes. But, while the literal meaning of death is certainly relevant here, it is also limiting.

Death is a transformational process, both literally and metaphorically. Consider the leaves on the trees in autumn, for example. As they change to brilliant shades of orange, red, and yellow, they slowly begin to wither and die. Eventually, they turn brown and fall to the ground. The trees appear to be "dead," but they are merely dormant. As the fallen leaves decompose, they return to the soil, where they provide nutrients for other plants and trees that will use them to grow and flourish. The following spring, these same trees sprout new leaves that are similar, but different. In the same way, death is a process of releasing the old to embrace the new.

When we shift our focus from the literal to the metaphorical, we find Anubis standing there, just between the shadow and the light. Death, like the turning of the seasons, is transformative, and transformation is what Anubis, as Lord of Death, embodies. By extension, his strong association with death also means that he is Lord of Transformation. Most statues and artistic representations portray him clothed in black with gold adornments (see figure on page 17). While this is definitely aesthetically pleasing, there's a reason he's portrayed this way. Symbolically, he stands on the liminal boundary between darkness and light, death and life. With his inner light, he leads the way out of the darkness and into the light.

Anubis functions as a guide to lead us through the deaths we all experience throughout our lives. He aligns well with the tarot card of Death, because transformation lies at the heart of what he represents. He has a funny way of showing up when people need him, often in the most chaotic and difficult periods in life. I have sought him time after time to lead me through particularly difficult times in my life, calling out his name in the dark hours of the night when I have felt at my weakest.

This doesn't mean that change won't happen, and it doesn't necessarily mean that things will get easier. But it does mean that, if you ask for his assistance, it's possible that Anubis will be there to guide you and support you through these transformational periods. He can help you realize that you are strong enough to get through them.

Metaphorically speaking, life is full of death—illness, trauma, job changes, moving, relationship problems, financial woes, unexpected tragedies, natural disasters, and more. We sometimes cannot predict these metaphorical deaths or stop them from happening, and they can sometimes continue for some time, even for a lifetime. The results of these experiences can vary. They may bring something better, something that was much needed, or they may have been meant to strengthen us.

When the recent pandemic took hold of the world, I lost my job. The company that I worked for at the time had to make difficult decisions to cut "unnecessary" jobs in order to save money and protect the company.

I spent the next year out of work, relying on unemployment benefits and state and federal aid to get by, and for access to the healthcare that I needed. On top of that, health challenges arose that demanded much of my time, as well as money that I simply did not have. Finally, I found a job that afforded me stability and flexibility. But when I look back on who I was before this happened, I see changes in myself. I am much more resilient than I was. Stronger. Was it horrible? Absolutely, without a shadow of a doubt. Would I choose to go through it again? No. But the truth is that it was a transformation, a death, that changed part of who I am and how I navigate the world.

Take a moment to think of who you were as a child. Think of all the things you liked doing. Where did you play? What games did you like? What were your favorite toys? Who were your friends? Think of the kind of child you were. Were you shy? Outgoing? A bit of a troublemaker? Hyperactive?

Now think about who you are now. How many of those things still hold true? Likely, many of them have changed. Of course, as adults, most of us do not "play" in the same sense that we did as children, but we do have hobbies and interests that we enjoy—a form of play, if you will. And the truth remains that we all change throughout our lives. Even from year to year as adults, our lives change drastically and I am willing to bet that you are a different person now than you used to be. This is transformation. This is a death of sorts. Part of you "died" (transformed) so that you could become the person you are now.

As you continue your journey exploring Anubis and building your relationship with him, you may actively seek help from him as Lord of Transformation. As Great Shaman, he can act as a guide during any shadow work that you may choose to undertake. In Chapter 17, we'll look more closely at how he can support you in this kind of work.

Prayer for Transformation

Hail to the Lord of Death!
Obsidian Lord of Night,
He who stands between worlds.

Anubis, Lord of Death,
Light in the Dark,
Shroud me in your cloak
That I may emerge transformed.

Hail Anubis, Lord of Death!
Transformer,
Teach me the meaning of transformation
That I may embrace its meaning
And enhance my life.

Journal Prompts

- Reflect on the idea of death as a transformation. What does it mean to you?

- What "deaths" have you experienced in your life?

- In what ways have you changed throughout your life?

CHAPTER 4

Master Healer and Chief Embalmer

*When he died, all things soft and beautiful and bright
would be buried with him.*

MADELINE MILLER, *THE SONG OF ACHILLES*

Medicine was not an unknown art to the ancient Egyptians, nor was it necessarily far off from many practices that still exist today. Modern archeologists have found mummies with extensive dental work, amputations, and surgeries that appear to have been performed and healed long before their deaths. Surgical tools were used that are still in use today in modern medicine, as well as prosthetic limbs, often made of wood.

Magick was also a huge component of ancient Egyptian medicine. The amulets and talismans used to invoke energies and powers for a particular purpose were extremely important. Perhaps most important of all, however, was the use of words. In ancient Egyptian magick, words held power. Speaking the right incantation with the correct pronunciation and intonation could invoke deities, banish illness, and cure ailments. Certain gods were invoked for certain purposes—not only for healing, but for protection.

As Master Healer and Chief Embalmer, Anubis—and likewise his priests—needed extensive knowledge of human anatomy, as well as that of animals like cats, dogs, cattle, crocodiles, and other animals that were often mummified as well. Embalming and mummification required a knowledge of the various parts of the human body, including where various organs were located and how they were connected, so that they could be properly preserved or, in some cases, removed without mutilating or destroying the body. This was an important part of Egyptian death culture, because it was believed that the soul returned to its body in the afterlife. Thus the body needed to be carefully prepared for the soul's return. Being a priest embalmer also required knowledge of the materials, herbs, and minerals that worked best to dry and preserve the tissues and organs of the body. Because of this, it is said that Anubis's priests were also well versed in herbalism and herbal healing.

The Art of Embalming

In the earliest days of Egyptian civilization, bodies were buried directly into the sand, allowing the extreme dry heat to preserve them naturally. Over time, the Egyptians discovered what worked and what didn't to help this process along. They developed the art of embalming into an exact science, and Anubis was the mastermind behind the process. We saw in chapter 2 that, when Osiris was murdered at the hands of his brother, it was Anubis who invented embalming so that his body could be preserved and he could be brought back to life. The Egyptians sought to reenact this mythological event so that they, too, could be reborn.

The embalming process was quite complex, and it was no quick, easy task. It involved a lot of time—the lengthy ritual required seventy days—and a lot of resources. Because of its ritual aspects, embalmers were also priests, and they wore masks representing Anubis's head as they worked to invoke his guidance. Embalming began with the removal of the brain, a less important organ to the Egyptians. It was carefully removed through the nose in separate small pieces to avoid damaging the face. Other major organs were then removed and placed into four special jars called *canopic jars*—one for the lungs, one for the liver, one for the intestines, and one for the stomach. Each jar featured the head of one of the sons of Horus on the lid. The only organ that remained in the body was the heart, as it was believed that the heart was the seat of the soul.

One of the four canopic jars depicted a god named Duamutef, which means "he who praises his mother." Duamutef was the protector of the stomach of the deceased. He was generally portrayed as a canid head atop the jar, although sometimes he was depicted separately as a mummified figure with a canid head, sometimes standing and sometimes kneeling. His skin was either black or dark green to represent the afterlife and rebirth. Green may seem like an odd choice here, but Osiris is often depicted as a mummified figure with green skin as well, again representing rebirth.

After the removal of the organs, bodies were covered in natron—sodium carbonate decahydrate—a naturally occurring mineral similar to salt that is extremely dehydrating. This was mined in several places near Egypt, one of which was called Wadi Natrun (now in modern-day Libya), which is where the compound gets its name. Natron was commonly found at the bottom of dry lake beds and in salt flats. Packets of natron were also placed inside the body's cavities to ensure that it was dried both inside and out. The whole process required a lot of the mineral.

Once the bodies had been completely dried, the natron packets were removed and the body was covered in resin and other preservatives in order to harden it so it would retain its appearance and shape. Sacred oils were then used to anoint the body and it was filled with wrappings and other materials in places where the skin had sunk in to make it appear more lifelike.

Imiut, one of the oldest and best-known epithets for Anubis, translates roughly as He Who Is in the Place of Embalming, or perhaps He Who Is in Mummy Wrappings, referring to his role in embalming and mummification. The name dates back as far as 2700 BCE, and was used throughout the entirety of ancient Egyptian history. It provides a perfect description of Anubis as he watches and guides the priests who performed the embalming and mummification rituals. These priests were extremely important and their hands were guided by Anubis himself, so giving him an epithet associated with the process made sense.

Imiut was also the name of an object sacred to Anubis that was often kept at embalming sites as a sort of representational talisman. This was a pole stuck into a pot with the hide of an animal, possibly a cow, hanging from it. It is thought to represent Hesat, a cow goddess who is sometimes described as Anubis's mother. This sacred symbol represents healing and rebirth, both acts sacred to embalmers and physicians. When Hesat squirted her sacred milk onto the imiut, it acquired powers that helped in the transformation process of the body.

Mummification and Burial

Once the body was well preserved, it was prepared for burial or entombment. This important part of the preservation process helped provide the deceased with the space they would need upon awakening in the afterlife. The body was wrapped in linens—the "mummy wrappings" we think of today. These linens were not easy to make, and sometimes hundreds of meters were required to wrap one body. Mummified remains of both humans and animals have been found wrapped in these linens. For humans, the fingers, toes, hands, and feet were wrapped separately first, then the legs and then the torso. Finally, the entire body was encased in the wrappings.

Small amulets, including those depicting Anubis, were woven between the layers of the wrappings as a means of protection. These often included carvings of scarabs, a sacred animal and symbol in ancient Egypt. Scarabs were placed in the linens over the heart to ensure that the soul would return to its body in the afterlife instead of being rejected. Another protective amulet wrapped within the linens depicted the Eye of Horus, representing the sun and the moon.

Probably one of the most important parts of the post-death preparations for the afterlife was called the Opening of the Mouth, which was performed by both Khenti-Amentiu and Anubis. Priests wore jackal masks depicting Anubis while performing this ceremony, which was one of the last rites completed before the body was entombed. During this ritual, priests touched various points on the body with a sacred tool—a long pole with a forked end—completing its "reanimation" and awakening the senses of the eyes, ears, nose, and mouth, the point through which the spirit re-entered the body. Touching each sense organ with this tool prepared the body to receive the spirit of the deceased once again and

Anubis poised and ready to defend a burial site.

Priests of Anubis performing the Opening of the Mouth ritual using sacred tool.

enabled the spirit to reconnect with it. The deceased was also anointed with various oils during this ritual and they were offered as libations to Anubis and as welcoming "gifts" to the deceased as well.

Once this ritual was completed, a death mask was placed over the wrapped face. These were ornate masks, often covered with gold, that showed the deceased's best features to help identify them. The mummified body was then placed into a coffin and then into a sarcophagus in the tomb, along with the canopic jars containing the deceased's organs and the riches and possessions that would support them in the afterlife. Food was also buried with them so that, upon awakening in the afterlife, they would have something to eat.

Anubis preparing the mummy of a worker, identified as either Amennakht or Nebenmaat.

This elaborate process was clearly not something that everyone could afford, however. It took an incredible amount of natron, which, although mined nearby, was a limited resource. Add to that the cost of the wrappings, the embalming fluids, and the valuable time of the embalming priests, as well as the cost of a coffin, a sarcophagus, a tomb, and all the riches to fill it, and you can see why this privilege was usually reserved for pharaohs and the nobility. On rare occasions, commoners could earn the right to be embalmed, but they were more often buried in shallow graves, their bodies wrapped carefully in shrouds.

Great Shaman

Anubis's role in healing goes beyond the physical realm. He's also referred to as Great Shaman, although the word "shaman" did not originate in Egypt. In fact, shamanism is a worldwide practice not exclusive to any one region and the word "shaman" has found its way into the English language to describe practices used in many cultures throughout history.

We can see evidence of Anubis's own shamanic journey in the origin myth by Plutarch. He was essentially abandoned as a child and ended up an orphan. He had to reunite with his inner self and go within to heal. Processing and healing from this as a human might have taken years, or even decades. But the gods work differently than we do, and this is one of the many lessons that Anubis teaches us—the importance of the journey to healing old pains and inner wounds that have stuck with us over many years. We see this in his role as Great Shaman.

There obviously is and always will be a literal dimension to death. But, as we have seen, there is also a more symbolic meaning associated with change and transformation that is embraced by many spiritual practices. Life can be full of chaos, upheavals, and change. But as a result of these "deaths," transformation can occur. Life can become something better, or at least something that we need at a particular time.

In my own life, I have had plenty of chaotic ups and downs that needed balancing and healing. And while I can't rightly say that Anubis can take all of the credit for the transformations that resulted, I can say, without a doubt, that he had a great impact on my own journey through the darkness. I would not have been able to get through years of trauma and abuse if it hadn't been for him. I wouldn't have been able to get through my teenage years as an LGBTQ youth in a small conservative community. I wouldn't have made it through financial struggles and physical and mental health challenges. Although I can't give Anubis all of the credit, I know that having him in my life to guide me through these "deaths" has been transformational for me.

If you've gone through any kind of trauma, abuse, abandonment, or difficult life experiences from which you need to heal, Anubis can be there with you to act as a shamanic guide. This doesn't mean that you don't have to do the work, because you do. But having a guide to help you along the way can ease the process by giving you the protection, support, and courage you need to face all of that inner work.

There are many paths to healing inner pain, and none of them are necessarily better than others. (We'll examine shadow work more closely in chapter 17.) There have been countless books, articles, talks, videos, and blog posts written about healing. It may take a fair amount of time and effort—and a bit of trial and error—to find what works best for you. And what works for one person may not necessarily work for others. But embarking on a healing journey with Anubis can be an incredibly powerful experience.

As Great Shaman, Anubis stands in the darkness, radiating his golden light to show you the way. He reaches into the depths of the darkness, helping you find your pain, pulling it forward so that you can confront it. His realm is the astral plane, the spirit realm, the place you go to during dreams and journeying. As psychopomp, protector, and shaman, he can guide you to the messages you need to hear and to the spaces you need to be in in order to heal.

Prayer for Guidance and Protection

Dua Anpu!
Walk with me.
Guard me on my path.
Shroud me in your dark cloak of protection.

Always be sure to give thanks after you have petitioned Anubis. I highly recommend making an offering as a token of gratitude. This can be as simple as burning incense or something larger and grander. You'll find more about offerings in chapter 13.

Journal Prompts

- Write down your thoughts about the embalming process. What do you think about all the preparatory work ancient Egyptians put into the process?

- Are there areas of your life that Anubis, as Great Shaman, could help heal?

CHAPTER 5

Psychopomp and Guide

"Do not fear . . . I will guide you through my world of deep magic,
strange gods, and gruesome monsters. I will show you how my people,
the ancient Egyptians, prepared the dead for eternal life."

VICKY ALVEAR SHECTER, *ANUBIS SPEAKS!*

A *psychopomp* is a deity or spirit who guides the souls of the deceased into the afterlife. This includes deities like Anubis, Hermes, Hekate, Charon, the Valkyries, and Morgana, but can also include figures like the Archangel Michael, Jesus, angels, and the Japanese *shinigami*. In some practices, the role is filled by an animal—including birds or dogs, explaining why we often see figures like Anubis and Hekate associated with canids. The term "hellhounds" comes to mind here. In *The Chilling Adventures of Sabrina*, a psychopomp takes the form of a sparrow who drags witches to the Underworld if they spend too much time in the spirit realm. Psychopomps greet souls upon death and lead them to the appropriate place in the afterlife—however that is viewed in a particular religious or spiritual practice.

Traditionally, it wasn't the job of a psychopomp to make any kind of judgment on souls. It didn't matter what kind of life the deceased had lived. In the end, everyone had to make the journey from the body into the afterlife, whatever that may have held for them. Sometimes this was an ugly, harsh truth that had to be accepted. In many cultures, people prayed to the gods and spirits of the Underworld for protection and guidance to ease this transition, and spent much of their time in this life trying to appease these spirits and deities so as not to be afraid. Likewise, it wasn't Anubis's direct role to judge the dead, although he was the one who presided over the Weighing of the Heart ceremony that decided their fate. Although he was the one who actually conducted the ceremony, he didn't make the final judgment on the deceased's soul.

Anubis is well known for being a guide for the souls of the departed, leading them down the long road through the Underworld to the Hall of Two Truths, where their souls were judged, and hopefully to the Field of Reeds—sometimes known as the Field of Offerings—the place of bliss in which they could enjoy a prosperous afterlife.

The Duat

Depictions of the Underworld vary widely across different cultures. In some, it was a cold, dark place full of fear and turmoil. In others, it was a rather empty place. In ancient Egyptian lore, the name for the Underworld was the *Duat*, or perhaps the *Tuat*. The Duat, the sacred land of the dead and Anubis's realm, was a vast, expansive place that included a multitude of areas. Some were thought to be beautiful, while others were seen as more gruesome and harsh. Souls were sent to a particular place based on the judgment they received in the Hall of Two Truths.

Although he wasn't the only deity who existed in the Duat, Anubis was referred to in many ancient texts, especially by the Greeks, as Pharaoh of the Underworld, indicating both his status and importance in death and his role in the afterlife. Long before Osiris's resurrection, Anubis presided over the court of the Underworld and held dominion there. This, together with his connection to the sun, puts him in an elevated position of authority, sovereignty, and kingship. We'll talk about this in more detail in chapter 9.

The Duat was not necessarily a place to fear. While other religions and spiritual practices have pictured it as a place of eternal damnation, torment, and fire, the majority of ancient Egyptians understood that the

Underworld was simply where you went upon death. Of course, it didn't mean sunshine and rainbows for all eternity, not by any means, because there was still the distinct possibility that your soul might be deemed unworthy. In this case, it would either be consumed by the demon god Ammit the Devourer, or you would be consigned to an eternity of suffering. But this had little to do with the understanding of the Duat as simply the place where you went when you died.

Upon death, the soul entered the Duat and began a long journey that wasn't particularly interesting or enjoyable, but was necessary. On this journey, the deceased had to pass through a series of twelve gates, each guarded by an entity—a god, a goddess, or some other spirit—many of whom were gruesome and fearful creatures. In order to pass safely, the deceased had to name these entities appropriately and recite a spell or incantation. Yet another reason to spend a lot of your time in this life preparing for the afterlife! These gates also corresponded to the hours of the night, during which the sun god Ra pulled his boat across the Underworld and battled the serpent demon Apep (in Greek, *Apophis*). By following the path and passing through these gates, souls essentially traversed the "nighttime," navigating the darkness and, ideally, emerging into the light.

Entering the Duat, the underworld of Anubis, on the barque of Ra.

One common epithet of Anubis is Lord of the Sacred Land (*Neb-Ta-Djeser*), likely a reference to the necropoli, the sacred burial grounds found throughout Egypt. This epithet reinforces once again that Anubis was a deity associated with the dead and with the Duat. He was called upon to watch over the dead, in both body and spirit, and the necropoli were an important part of his domain. Not all places of burial were large, elaborate tombs buried deep within pyramids and temples, however. These were saved for the kings and pharaohs who could afford them—and, according to the Egyptians, deserved them because of their association with divinity. Many necropoli were based in areas where pyramids were built so that other nobles and lesser officials could be buried near the royal tombs.

Some necropoli were smaller cemeteries dedicated to the burial of common folk. Although these are now hard to find because they aren't marked by elaborate structures like pyramids, Anubis was nonetheless their guardian and protector as well. As psychopomp, he guided the spirits of the dead through the afterlife to the Duat—hopefully to the bountiful land called the Field of Reeds.

Another common epithet for Anubis that reinforces his connection to the Duat is Opener of Ways. This derives from the ancient Egyptian name for Wepwawet, *Apuat,* whom we met in chapter 1. Some think that Wepwawet, as the son of either Set and Nephthys or Osiris and Nephthys, is Anubis's brother. His appearance differed slightly from Anubis's, however, as he was portrayed with the head of a wolf with either gray or white skin to differentiate him from other jackal-headed deities. Moreover, he is sometimes portrayed as seated, a posture not commonly seen in depictions of Anubis.

As Opener of Ways, Anubis appears in his role as a guide for the dead, a role also fulfilled by Wepwawet. In fact, as we saw in chapter 1, some argue that Wepwawet and Anubis are one and the same, although today most agree that they are two distinct gods, based on their different origins and portrayals. Nonetheless, it's entirely possible that Wepwawet and Anubis were seen as different aspects or interpretations of the same canid-headed god by ancient Egyptians because of their nearly identical roles. In fact, Wepwawet and Anubis were often depicted together on coffins and tomb walls as two jackals or jackal-headed figures facing each other. Over time, however, the importance of Wepwawet faded and Anubis assimilated his role as he gained popularity. When this happened, Anubis assumed the name of Opener of Ways.

Prayer for a Departed Soul

Hail Anubis Psychopompos!
He who protects,
He who leads the souls of the departed to the afterlife,
He who walks with the weary traveler.
Pharaoh of the Underworld,
Bless this departed soul, this weary traveler.
Though this phase of their journey is over,
May they remember that this is just the beginning.
Great Pharaoh of the Underworld,
Be with them on their journey to what lies next.
Walk with them, comfort them, guide them.
May they find their way to their next destination.
May they find peace, comfort, and solace in your presence,
Forever guided by your inner light.
Hail Anubis!

Journal Prompts

- What other psychopomp figures can you name? How are they similar to or different from Anubis?

- What other depictions of the Underworld do you know about? How are they similar to or different from the Duat?

CHAPTER 6

Master of Scales and Weigher of Souls

After a long journey down a winding pathway, I find myself standing in a large hall. It is quite dark, although I can still see well. Torches line the walls of stone; shadows dance across the floor. At one end is a throne on which sits Osiris, Lord of the Underworld. He watches me silently as I approach the center of the room, where a large ornate scale stands, covered with etchings of mysterious symbols and protective spells. I can sense that it is as old as time itself. It echoes of power and of truth.

Standing next to the scales is the Lord of Death himself—Anubis, Anpu, Master of Scales. His presence fills the room. In one hand, he holds a staff topped by an ankh. In the other, he holds a simple but brilliant white feather. His golden eyes gaze upon me, and I feel that they pierce my soul. I do not feel afraid. I know why I am here, and I am ready. "Let us begin," he says with a gentle nod.

<small>Anubis to me during a vision</small>

One of the greatest symbols associated with Anubis is the scale. I'm not talking about a scale like the one in your bathroom or on your kitchen counter. I'm talking about an old balance scale with two platforms suspended from a central point—the kind of scale used to compare the weight of two objects. What does this scale have to do with Anubis? The answer lies in his role as Weigher of Souls.

As we have seen, ancient Egyptians believed that, upon death, their souls traveled down a great pathway through a series of gateways that were each connected to a particular deity who required a particular spell and utterance in order to pass. Anubis was the guide on this journey, which ended at the Hall of Two Truths, where the final judgment took place. Osiris sat watching all this happen, but, let's be honest, not really doing anything. The ibis-headed god of knowledge and writing, Thoth, stood near to act as scribe and record the judgment. Forty-two other gods and goddesses, representing the forty-two Laws of Ma'at, sat waiting to hear what was said. But it was Anubis who stood in the center holding the scale.

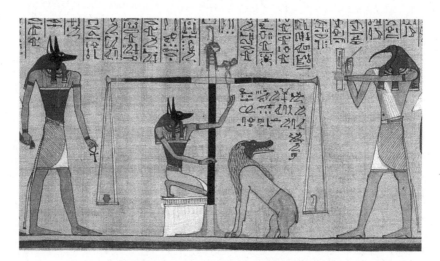

The heart being weighed against the feather of Ma'at.

As we saw in chapter 4, in ancient Egypt, the heart was considered the seat of the soul, so it was the heart that was weighed against the Feather of Ma'at, the goddess of truth, justice, and equity, and balancer of all things. She was typically represented as a woman with outstretched wings and a brilliantly white ostrich feather on her head. She represented the principle or ideal of what it meant to "live a good life." Egyptians believed that their lives needed to have enough *ma'at* to counter the chaos of earthly existence.

Ma'at over the scales as Anubis weighs the heart.

It was Anubis who placed the deceased's heart on the scale and oversaw the weighing process. Before he did so, the deceased stood before him and made a Declaration of Innocence in front of those present. If the heart being weighed was lighter than the Feather of Ma'at, the deceased was deemed to have lived a life worthy of reaching the Field of Reeds, the peaceful space in the afterlife where souls spent their days enjoying abundance, prosperity, and joy. If it was heavier than the Feather of Ma'at, it was deemed unfit and fed to Ammit the Devourer—a particularly gruesome fate, since to destroy the heart was to destroy the soul.

The Forty-Two Laws of Ma'at

According to ancient Egyptian religion, the world was governed by forty-two principles of truth, harmony, order, justice, and balance that everyone was required to uphold in order to lead a good life. These made up the Declaration of Innocence that the deceased recited in front of those present in the Hall of Two Truths. These were stated as affirmations, declaring the ways in which the deceased had lived their lives so that they could end their journey in the Field of Reeds. The Feather of Ma'at represented the entirety of these laws, and it was against this feather that the heart was weighed. Thus, as Master of Scales, Anubis functioned as the upholder of these laws.

The forty-two affirmations, or laws, comprise the essentials for living a life of integrity, much like the principles and commandments that have governed other religions and cultures across time. They are generally given as follows:

1. I have not done wrong.

2. I have not robbed.

3. I have not stolen.

4. I have not slain people.

5. I have not destroyed a food offering.

6. I have not reduced measures.

7. I have not stolen a god's property.

8. I have not told lies.

9. I have not stolen food.

10. I was not sullen.

11. I have not fornicated with a fornicator.

12. I have not caused anyone to weep.

13. I have not dissembled.

14. I have not transgressed.

15. I have not done grain-profiteering.

16. I have not robbed a parcel of land.

17. I have not discussed secrets.

18. I have brought no lawsuits.

19. I have not disputed at all about property.

20. I have not had intercourse with a married woman.

21. I have not seduced another man's wife.

22. I have not wrongly copulated.

23. I have not struck terror.

24. I have not transgressed.

25. I have not been hot-tempered.

26. I have not been neglectful of truthful words.

27. I have not cursed.

28. I have not been violent.

29. I have not confounded truth.

30. I have not been impatient.

31. I have not discussed.

32. I have not been garrulous about matters.

33. I have not done wrong; I have not done evil.

34. I have not disputed the king.

35. I have not waded in the water.

36. My voice was not loud.

37. I have not cursed a god.

38. I have not made extollings.

39. I have not harmed the bread-ration of the gods.

40. I have not stolen the Khenef-cakes from the Blessed.

41. I have not stolen Hefnu-cakes of a youth, nor have I fettered the god of my town.

42. I have not slain sacred cattle.

Of course, modern life is vastly different from the lives of ancient Egyptians. Modern technology, for one, has changed the way we live our lives. We no longer have cattle or grain to declare innocence over (well, most of us don't). We don't mummify our dead, nor do we build elaborate tombs and fill them with riches and gold. Moreover, our values have changed. All that being said, however, there is still a lot of value in these forty-two laws that is applicable today, and these essential principles of living a good life still survive in the fields of psychology and sociology, and in various spiritual practices.

If you plan to do any kind of work with Anubis, keep these principles in mind. No one can tell you how to live your life. You have the freedom to do with it what you will. But my interactions with Anubis have shown me that he does expect a certain level of integrity and authenticity. He values compassion, and does not tolerate any kind of hatred or unnecessary cruelty. He expects you to keep your word. If you make a promise to do something, you had better do it. This doesn't mean that you suddenly have to become a "goody goody." But it does mean that you should try to commit to doing what you say. You should strive to treat others in the way they deserve to be treated—and, following the Golden Rule, the way you'd like to be treated yourself.

Moreover, you shouldn't allow others to do these things to you. I think that there is also power in this. It really says a lot about your character when you stand up for yourself. My experiences have shown me that Anubis values those who are independent, live their truth, and stand up for themselves.

Prayer to the Master of Scales

Anubis, Master of Scales,
Weigher of Souls,
Grant me the vision, knowledge, and wisdom
To live a life of integrity, honesty, and truth;
To strive to be compassionate and caring;
To live my truth;
To live my purpose.
Hail Anubis!

Journal Prompts

- Do you think the forty-two Laws of Ma'at are relevant today?

- Which of them do you find most relevant? Are there any that you do not find relevant?

- If you were to "modernize" the list, what would you add or change?

CHAPTER 7

The Great Watcher

In a far-off land in a small village now lost to time, an elderly man watches the sunset, knowing it may be his last. As the sun illuminates the mountains, he smiles with bittersweet sorrow, closes his eyes, and whispers: "Anubis, be with me."

A thousand years later, a woman sits alone in her home. She knows that she will be killed if anyone discovers she still worships the old gods. She reverently holds an ankh. It is all she has left, but it is enough for her. Quietly, she kisses it and whispers: "Anubis, be with me."

A young teen, I sit in my bedroom crying because I don't want to go to school anymore. It has become an uncomfortable place full of teasing and torment about who I am—what I look like, whom I love. Desperate to feel some kind of comfort and protection, I whisper: "Anubis, be with me."

ANUBIS TO ME DURING A MEDITATION

Across time and across space, we all share a bond with Anubis, the Great Watcher. He protects the spirits of both the living and the dead. He guards the spirits of the deceased from attack and guides them on their journey through the afterlife. Many of his epithets reflect these roles. One of the most famous of these is He Who Is upon His Mountain

(*Tepy-Dju-Ef*), which portrays him perched up high and keeping a watchful eye out for enemies and predators.

In ancient Egypt, Anubis was associated more specifically with watching over cemeteries and tombs, although today his role seems to relate to any scenario in which he is watchful. As the Great Watcher, his eyes pierce through darkness and shadow and see all. Likewise *Episkopos*, an epithet given to him by the Greeks, meant "watcher" or "observer," again reflecting his protective nature as guardian, while *Phouros*, also given to him by the Greeks, meant "guardian" and referred to him specifically as the protector of Osiris. All these epithets tend to reinforce his role as a watchful protector and guardian.

The Color of Protection

Black was a sacred color in ancient Egypt that was associated not only with death and protection but also with fertility and regeneration. The word for black in ancient Egyptian was *kem*. In fact, the name for the ancient land we now call Egypt was *Kemet*, meaning "black land," because the soil around the Nile was black from periodic flooding, making it incredibly fertile. This is the origin of the word *Kemeticism*, the practice of the religious, spiritual, and sometimes cultural values of ancient Egypt. Those who practice Kemeticism are called Kemetics, or sometimes Kemetic practitioners.

In addition to being a protective color, black was also the color of death and rebirth, and that is why Anubis is often portrayed with black skin. He watched over the souls of those under his care, ushering them to the afterlife and protecting them along their journey. Moreover, most people in ancient Egypt prayed to Anubis for protection throughout their lifetimes, in hopes that they would be guided to the afterlife upon death. As we have seen, his image and name were inscribed on tombs and adorned sarcophagi and coffins, while statues of him watched over tombs to ensure the safe passage of the deceased to the Underworld.

Black has been considered a protective color for thousands of years. In witchcraft, black is associated with protection and shielding. Witches frequently dress in black and use black accessories, which is why they are often portrayed wearing black robes in popular media today. Although these portrayals are often gross exaggerations, their origin lies in the fact that witches historically wore black to protect themselves from the energies with which they worked. Black helped to protect and contain their own energy, while simultaneously shielding them from any unwanted energies surrounding them. Black is arguably the most sacred color to witches.

Many of the tools of witchcraft are also black. Witches use black candles for protection spells. Their cauldrons are black in order to contain the ingredients and the spell within. They use black crystals like obsidian, jet, black tourmaline, and onyx to protect themselves from unwanted energies, and often have black cats and ravens as spirit allies or familiars. All these tools have a spiritual and magickal connection to the color black.

Partly because of this association, many witches work with Anubis today to protect themselves while doing spell work or during astral travel. Indeed, Anubis's role as Great Watcher extends to astral travel or to any other kind of journey. As Great Shaman and psychopomp, he guides those who travel through the spirit realm. If you plan to work in this way, Anubis can walk with you and help you to find your way.

Guardian of the Marginalized

According to Plutarch's myth, Anubis himself was one of the marginalized. Conceived by means of deceit and trickery, he was rejected by his own family. Thus he became essentially a homeless orphan, who was then adopted by Isis and Osiris. If Anubis had been human, he most likely would have felt alone and unwanted, even unloved. It is hard for us to know how he would have felt, however, because the gods do not have the same emotions that we do. Nonetheless, we can at least surmise that these experiences would have affected him in some way. Given his predisposition for watching over souls, it's safe to assume that he might have had a soft spot for those who felt lost, lonely, and abandoned.

Perhaps because of his own experience, Anubis watches over the marginalized and those who are unwanted or unloved. No matter who you are, as long as you approach him with integrity and respect, he will watch over you and may grant you protection. He welcomes everyone

(I do mean that) and, as I know from my own experiences, he supports all individuals regardless of gender, race, sexual orientation, ethnicity, background, ability, or upbringing. One of the most famous pharaohs, Tutankhamun, was physically disabled, and yet his tomb contained one of the largest depictions of Anubis ever found.

The population of ancient Egypt was more diverse than you might think. It included native Egyptians, as well as Greeks, Romans, and Persians who came to inhabit the region—although not necessarily in a friendly manner. Cities along the coast of the Mediterranean and along the Nile became hubs for visitors from foreign lands, bringing with them their own gods and goddesses, their own cultural values, and their own life stories. Rich and poor, commoner and royalty, thinkers and builders, artists and designers, farmers, and everyone in between came to Egypt from far-off lands.

Almost all cultures at the time openly welcomed same-sex and interracial couples. In fact, a spell written thousands of years ago that survives in the *Greek Magical Papyri* invokes Anubis and Hermes in a same-sex love spell between two women. Nyankh-khnum and Khnum-hotep, two high officials in the pharaoh's court who lived between 2500 BCE and 2300 BCE, were buried together in the same tomb. We don't know exactly what their relationship was, but many now accept that they were, in fact, lovers. The tomb depicts the two of them touching noses, a sign in the artwork of the time of an intimate kiss. They were important enough to be buried together and granted all of the same protections and guidance in the afterlife as everyone else.

The point is that what matters most is the manner in which you approach Anubis and the life that you live—not who you are, where you're from, or whom you love. Anubis watches over anyone who wishes to feel his embrace and shelter under his protective cloak. When times are dark, he will act as guide, his eyes shining bright in the darkness to illuminate the way. He remains the light when all else seems dark and cold.

In the later years of ancient Egypt, anyone could make the journey to the afterlife—not just pharaohs—as long as they could pass a series of trials by which they were judged for the life they had lived. And Anubis guarded and guided anyone and everyone who passed through the Underworld. He watched over their journey regardless of who they were. He protected all souls—right up until the time when their hearts were weighed —and beyond that into that afterlife.

Petitioning Anubis

Anubis can be petitioned for protection for a variety of reasons. During times when you may be feeling unsafe or alone, he can be there to protect you. He can be the guardian you need when you fall prey to your fears. He can also soothe and calm your anxious nerves when you are overwhelmed by life's challenges. Remember that he is the light within the darkness. He is able to see all when it seems that all is in shadow and guide you out of that darkness.

As we have seen, Anubis can also be called upon for protection during travel. I have found that he is a great protector "on the go." When I am going on any kind of trip, no matter how far it may be, I carry an amulet representing him with me, either on my person or near me in a bag or in my car. This doesn't have to be anything large or complicated. You can find simple trinkets online for a small price. I also like to wear a pendant depicting Anubis along with a smoky quartz bracelet that is good for any kind of travel or journey.

Anubis will also watch over you during any magickal work. As Master of Mysteries, he is very well versed in the realm of the occult and its secret lore (see chapter 8). These spaces are his domain, and he will protect you while you navigate them. Of course, he can also be petitioned for help in these workings. Trance work and journeying can be quite intense practices and, if you plan to do any of it, Anubis can be a powerful guide and protector to have with you. It's important always to have some kind of protection when doing any kind of journeying or trance work. And what better companion could you have at your side than the Great Shaman himself.

Anubis was petitioned for hundreds of years by Egyptians, Greeks, and Romans to help bridge the physical and ethereal worlds and communicate with the souls of the departed. Spells survive in the *Greek Magical Papyri* that called on him to bring forth the souls of the deceased so that casters could communicate with them. He was specifically petitioned for this because, as Lord of Death, he had access to all souls and because he provided excellent protection during this kind of work.

Today, many engage in communication with the dead, either in the form of ancestral work or mediumship. But these can both be dangerous practices. If you don't approach them with care, you can end up inviting in spirits or entities whose motives aren't exactly what you intended. It's vitally important to have protection during this kind of work. Many mediums, for example, have a guide with them at all times—an animal spirit ally, a deity, or another type of spirit guide. As the Great Watcher, Anubis stands quietly in the dark, offering a strong, solid presence. He can be called on for protection when needed, especially in situations in which you may not feel safe. Carry a stone like obsidian or black tourmaline with you and, when you feel that you need protection, you can call on him for help using one of the prayers found in this book, or one you have written yourself.

Prayer for the Marginalized

Anubis, Protector of All,
Guardian of the Lost,
Usher of Souls,
When my path feels dark,
Light the way with your eyes that pierce the darkness.
When I am feeling alone,
Be at my side and grant me comfort within your shroud.
Though my path is not easy
And it often feels like a life of solitude,
I find comfort and solace in your presence.

Journal Prompts

- What makes you feel protected and safe? What makes you feel unsafe?

- What symbols do you associate with protection?

- How can you incorporate Anubis into your protective spells?

CHAPTER 8

Master of Mysteries and Keeper of Keys

"I am the Master of Mysteries and guardian of the secrets of the world—seen and unseen. I am the Keeper of Keys to the doors leading to knowledge that lies beyond. I can unlock all the knowledge that you seek. Walk with me, and I will guide you through the door of your choosing. Take caution, however, for there are forces in this world and beyond that seek to harm and destroy."

ANUBIS TO ME DURING A MEDITATION

One of the greatest mysteries in life is death. What happens when we die? The world's greatest philosophers, scientists, thinkers, and religious leaders have contemplated this mystery since the dawn of time. Although no one seems to be able to come up with tangible, science-backed evidence that there is any kind of afterlife, many people are absolutely certain that there is. Yet our knowledge of exactly what happens when we die relies heavily on reports of near-death experiences and the insights of mystics, shamans, psychics, and healers who are in tune with the spirit world. We can't address this issue quantitatively, using measures like blood pressure or body temperature, because death takes us to a world beyond the physical body, into the realm of the soul.

Those who have had a near-death experience often tell of moving into a light, as if their soul begins to travel down a pathway into another world. Those who have gotten a glimpse of what lies on the other side often describe beautiful green scenery or a familiar place. Others tell of seeing loved ones—perhaps their parents, their siblings, a best friend, their grandparents, or even a lost pet. And some claim to have met angels or spirit guides who gave them some sort of message. No matter the difference in details, however, all these reports are strikingly similar—and that similarity gives you all the proof you need of their veracity. Just because we cannot quantitatively measure or confirm these experiences doesn't mean that they are not valid. *All* experiences are valid, and the fact that these are all so similar speaks to something extremely important.

As someone who believes in the existence of life after life and the survival of the soul, it's only natural for me to associate this great mystery and its exploration with Anubis. In his role as psychopomp, he leads us into the afterlife upon death, and reveals to us the secrets of the world around us and the greater mysteries of the spirit world. Death is just one facet of a world of spirits that is so vast and complex that we cannot begin to comprehend it. Connecting with these mysteries is not just about spirits, the afterlife, and divine guidance; it's also part of a journey that is full of energy and magick, full of spellcraft, legend, and lore. In fact, there is so much to discover and to know about the mysteries of the spirit world that you could dedicate your entire life to understanding it (as we witches do!) and still only have scratched the surface. But Anubis holds the master key that unlocks all doors—the ankh.

The Key-Bearer

One of the titles given to Anubis by the Greeks was Key-Bearer— *kleidukhos*. This epithet was used to describe other chthonic deities as well, like Persephone and Hekate. In fact, the term was associated with many deities who were connected to the Underworld, to death and rebirth, and to magick and the mysteries that surround us. Essentially, when you call on Anubis Kleidoukhos, you call upon the Keeper of Keys to these mysteries.

Another epithet that refers to Anubis's role as Keeper of Keys was *Anubis Psirinth*. This name was used by the Greeks to refer to a deity who held the keys to the realm of Hades—the Greek Underworld, which differed from the Duat in that it was thought to be a much darker place. While the Duat wasn't necessarily all happiness and sunshine, it was not always thought of as scary. Anubis Psirinth was invoked in the *Greek Magical Papyri* during binding spells and spells for protection.

Master of Secrets

Anubis's role as Master of Mysteries and Keeper of Keys was closely associated with his role as Chief Embalmer. The embalming process was not just about wrapping bodies up in linen. It consisted of carefully crafted rituals performed to ensure the preservation of the body through the spiritual significance of preserving the organs and preparing the deceased for what came afterward. The tools used and the practices involved were all considered sacred.

Anubis's association with this occult process was expressed in the epithet *Hery-Sesheta*—Master of Secrets, a title also given to priests and those who held some kind of administrative or leadership role in a temple. Those called by this name were generally seen as persons of authority or knowledge, and thus masters of secret lore. As a god of the dead, Anubis held the secrets to life and the afterlife, and all secrets of what lies beyond death. This certainly includes what some might consider to be the gruesome process of embalming, with which he was also associated. In fact, embalmers often wore masks of Anubis to honor him and to channel his spirit.

Those who combined these two roles—temple priests and those in charge of the embalming process—certainly needed to be knowledgeable in many areas. They needed to understand human anatomy and physiology, including how the body decays after death. They also needed to know how to preserve the body using herbs, minerals, and oils. The complicated and detailed process they performed could take over two months to complete and required that they understand the journey to the afterlife and how to help people get there through all of the painstaking steps in the preparatory stages. So it is easy to see how the epithet Master of Secrets can be applied to both Anubis and to temple priests.

Unless you are a funerary worker, embalming is probably far removed from your daily life. We don't embalm the dead as they once did in ancient Egypt. But the act of embalming as performed in ancient Egypt was a ritual that was akin to a lengthy spell, and if we think of it this way, it becomes easier to understand. Priests and embalmers always had a set space in which to do their work—a dedicated table in a dedicated room in a dedicated building. They anointed themselves with oils, used special cloths, and even wore ceremonial masks. Anubis himself was often invoked to oversee the process and, in many cases, the head embalmer was seen as channeling him. Their tools were carefully laid out in advance, each having its own significance and purpose. Incense and herbs were burned to create a sacred space and as an offering to the god. The process of embalming itself had very specific steps that needed to be carried out in a particular order to achieve the proper outcome. All the while, the officiants chanted or sang to invoke the desired intention—the preservation of the body and the preparation of the soul for the afterlife.

Doesn't this sound familiar? Witches use the same framework to craft their spells. They have a sacred space where they use tools, invoke spirits, and formulate their intentions in a specific manner to achieve a desired outcome. This is partially why Anubis has come to be associated with the occult, and why occult and metaphysical stores are often adorned with statues of him. It is also why the ankh has become a widely known symbol of all things occult and magickal. It is the master key to the mysteries and secrets of the spirit world—and Anubis is the keeper of that key.

Magick in Egypt

Magick, known as *heka* in ancient Egypt, was an integral part of life there. Moreover, it was not just seen as a spiritual practice; it was understood to be rooted in science and represented a deep body of knowledge to be studied and mastered. Magick was woven into every aspect of life in Egypt, including birth and death, medicine and agriculture, and business and learning. There was no division of "black magick" and "white magick," nor any characterization of magickal acts as "sorcery." Magick was simply a tool that was a part of everyday life and accessible to anyone who wished to use it. Not everyone did, however, as it required practice and training to which not everyone had access.

Words were arguably the most important feature of ancient Egyptian magick. Words held immense power. To know the true names of gods or goddesses, for example, meant to hold power over them and their dominions. Words were carved onto the walls of tombs and temples to imbue them with powerful protective spells. Spoken words were chanted by practitioners and prayed by worshippers as a means to carry out their intended meaning.

Amulets were also very potent magickal tools in ancient Egypt. They were often carved out of stone or perhaps resin that had been painted. They ranged in size, but were usually small enough to be worn or carried. They were charged with magickal spells and said to contain the power of the gods. These amulets were used by the living, but have also been found buried with the dead.

The deceased were often buried with amulets of Anubis in hopes of being granted his protection and guidance. They were sometimes placed in the linen wrappings of mummified bodies in order to weave their magick directly into the body. The living wore amulets depicting Anubis for the same purpose—protection and the assurance of guidance in the afterlife. These were either worn around the neck or the wrist, or kept somewhere safely tucked away on the person.

Shabtis—small statues carved out of wood, clay, stone, metal, or even glass—were magickal tools unique to ancient Egypt These figures were placed in tombs, sometimes by the hundreds. Why? Tradition had it that the families of the dead were supposed to bring food to them in their tombs. They were also supposed to take care of the tombs and make sacrificial offerings to the gods. When this came to be seen as an onerous task, people came up with a clever way to have someone else—or something else—do it for them. With the use of spells, they charged these figures with the tasks of maintaining the burial space, cleaning it, guarding it, and taking care of it. Sometimes a priest was hired to live nearby and take care of the offerings required, but shabtis took care of the rest. Each one had its own intended purpose.

A shabti of Yua, mother to the wife of Amenhotep III.

Divination

Divination is a powerful magickal practice used to interpret signs from the gods, peer into the future, gain insight into life, and receive messages from the spirit world. There were various divinatory practices in ancient Egypt, including scrying using water and oil or water and ink, fire-gazing, trance work, and dream interpretation. In Egypt during the time of Greek and Roman influence, Anubis was often petitioned to provide insight and knowledge through divination. Over a span of thousands of years, he was invoked in spell work ranging from protection, guidance, curses, necromancy, banishing, binding, and even love spells. As Keeper of Keys, he was petitioned to grant wisdom and unlock the doors to the mysteries of life and death.

There are many things in life that we do not fully understand and, despite the thousands of years we have spent trying, we just can't seem to solve the mystery of death. While there is a lot that we know and understand about death and what happens leading up to it, during it, and after it, we cannot know with absolute certainty what lies beyond it. There is so much more about death that we have yet to comprehend, and I have no doubt that we will continue on mankind's journey to understanding it better.

Magick is one of life's mysteries that, for those who practice it, we know for certain exists. We have seen firsthand the effects that it can have, but we truly cannot fully understand the intricacies of how it works. If you plan to embark on a journey of magick and mystery, however, Anubis can be your guide and your protector. Petition him for aid and he will lead you to the knowledge, resources, and experiences you need to reach your goal. Death, magick, and mystery all lie behind the doors to which Anubis holds the key.

Prayer to the Great Shaman

Anubis, Great Shaman,
Master of Mysteries and Guardian of Souls,
Guide me on this journey
As I travel to the realm of spirits.
Be at my side that I may not waver from my path.
Walk with me that I may be guided and protected.
With your golden eyes, pierce the darkness to guide the way.
With your dark cloak, protect me from all harm.
Hail Anubis!

Journal Prompts

- What is your experience with magick and divination?

- What mysteries and secrets of the universe do you wish to learn from Anubis?

CHAPTER 9

Anubis in the Modern World

The boundaries which divide Life from Death are at best shadowy and vague. Who shall say where one ends and the other begins?

Edgar Allan Poe

For thousands of years, Anubis has assumed many roles that go far beyond his role as the god of embalming. His reach has extended to encompass the mysteries of the world around us and how it is all connected and intertwined. He rests in many of the liminal spaces around us—between life and death, between light and darkness, between magick and mystery. Although he began as an ancient deity in the desert sands of Egypt, his influence has persisted across time and has grown beyond the borders of what we know as Egypt today—into Europe and other parts of the Mediterranean, and across the Middle East. And he remains a part of modern life.

In this chapter, we'll explore some of the ways in which his role has shifted, grown, and expanded, and how he has assumed roles far beyond those associateed with a god of death and embalming—perhaps without you even being aware that they are closely tied to him. This happened primarily through the blending of Anubis with gods from different pantheons.

In the course of its long history, ancient Egypt was conquered by the Persians, then the Greeks, and later the Romans. In fact, the now famous pyramids at Giza were already thousands of years old before the Greeks or Romans even thought about Egypt. During this period, the entire Mediterranean was a rather complicated region in which countries and kingdoms invaded each other frequently, thus blending their cultures. As these various groups attempted to understand one another's traditions, languages, and religious practices, they each made their own attempts at naming and interpreting the gods they found in the conquered lands. This, in fact, is where the name "Anubis" comes from. It was the closest the Greeks could come to *Anpu,* which was his Egyptian name.

From the 3rd-century Roman era, Anubis as defender of Osiris/Dionysus.

The Greeks and Romans tried hard in some cases to appease the conquered Egyptians by building new temples dedicated to their gods. In other cases, however, they tried to impose their own deities on the population. Sometimes they even tried to make direct associations between their gods and the gods of the conquered region. In fact, it became a popular practice to blend deities from more than one pantheon. Thus Amun and Ra were often associated with Zeus. Hathor, or perhaps Bast, was sometimes associated with Aphrodite. Horus was frequently associated with Apollo. Let's look at some of the ways in which they blended Anubis with gods from their own pantheons.

Anubis and Hermes

At first glance, it may seem peculiar that Anubis was associated with Hermes, the Greek messenger of the gods. Hermes was a trickster, while Anubis—although he had a witty and dry sense of humor—was not. When you consider their roles as psychopomp, however, it makes sense. Both Anubis and Hermes were tasked with ushering the souls of the dead into the afterlife, and this is the role that the Greeks co-opted and perpetuated.

Eventually, this association blended Hermes and Anubis into an entirely new deity, *Hermanubis*. I tend to see Hermanubis as being an aspect of both Anubis and Hermes, not necessarily as a separate deity in himself. But however you interpret this blended god, this is when Anubis's sphere of influence and his popularity began to expand quickly. He became so popular that the Romans later adopted Hermanubis into their own pantheon and his worship persisted for hundreds of years.

Hermanubis was said to be the son of Isis and Serapis, another Greco-Egyptian deity blended from a number of gods, including Osiris and Hades. Hermanubis is usually depicted as a robed man with the head of a dog and a solar disk between his ears to represent his divinity, sovereignty, and power. He was not only known as a psychopomp and healer, he was also associated with the Egyptian priesthood and acknowledged as a master of spells and magick. In one hand, he held the *kerykeion*, or caduceus, the winged staff with snakes coiled around it that is still used as a symbol to represent modern medicine. In the other hand, he often held a palm leaf, representing the cycles of life. Sometimes he was depicted wearing the winged sandals of Hermes. The largest known statue of Hermanubis resides in the collection of the Vatican Museum, but you can also find depictions of him in numerous artworks of the time.

Left: Anubis as Hermes, 1851. Right: Hermanubis statue, c. 1st–2nd century CE.

Anubis and Horus

An alternative theory of the origins of Hermanubis—and one that is just as compelling, if you ask me—is the blending of Horus and Anubis. Horus was often blended with many different deities, even within the Egyptian pantheon, not only to show his vast range of influence but also to depict him in various roles. He was an extremely important deity to the ancient Egyptians. In their language, the name for Horus was *Heru*, and the name for Anubis was *Anpu*. So the epithet *Heru-em-Anpu* can be interpreted as "Horus as Anubis," or, by extension, Horus assuming the role that Anubis plays. This later may have become Hermanubis, as the Greeks would call him.

Whether the Greeks misunderstood the meaning of the name Hermanubis or simply chose to take the name's meaning in a different direction is unknown. All we know is that, somehow, they ended up with a deity that blended Hermes and Anubis.

It's interesting to speculate about how Horus and Anubis might interact with one another, however. In Plutarch's myth of Anubis's origin, they are half-brothers. Horus is the kingly god of the skies, light, healing, and goodness. Anubis is the god of death and the Underworld. Horus is the light to Anubis's darkness. So the blending of the two into one deity yields one liminal god who has mastery over both life and death. He becomes a healer, but is still a psychopomp. As we have seen, Horus and Anubis were associated and paired together long before Hermanubis came to be, but this overt blending really expanded that association and took it further. And this interpretation persisted long into Greek and Roman times. This blended god was invoked for both benevolence and to instill fear, for both healing and death, representing the balance between light and life, and death and decay.

Rameses I, center, being led to the Underworld by Horus on the left and Anubis on the right.

Anubis and Wepwawet

As we saw in chapter 5, Anubis and Wepwawet were sometimes portrayed together as a jackal and a wolf facing each other, or as two canid-headed figures facing each other. Although they have sometimes been confused as the same deity portrayed twice, they were, in fact, two separate gods who were both known by the epithet Opener of Ways—Anubis from the north (his cult centered in Lower Egypt near the Nile delta in the north of Egypt) and Wepwawet from the south (his cult centered in Upper Egypt, the hillier and more mountainous regions to the south). They were portrayed in this way so that the deceased could find their way through the heavens from either the north or the south. By extension, Anubis came to be associated with the summer solstice and Wepwawet with the winter solstice, representing yet again the balance of light and darkness (see chapter 16).

Amulet of Wepwawet.

When portrayed with the Eye of Horus, representing the sun and the moon, Anubis and Wepwawet symbolized the four quarters and the four seasons of the year. Remember that, from Plutarch's perspective, Anubis was the son of Nephthys (darkness) who was brought up by Isis (light). Anubis thus stands between these two, representing that liminal space found at the horizon. He serves both the light and the darkness and resides in that middle plane. This is one reason why Anubis was seen as the guardian of the horizon. He is the truest liminal lord, in every sense of the word.

Anubis and Hekate

The portrayal of Anubis as a celestial being of both light and darkness leads easily to comparisons of him with Hekate, a Greek goddess of immense power and expansive reach. Hekate was the goddess of the crossroads of life and death, and of magick and mystery. But she was also thought to be a creatrix with influence over the elements, the directions, magick, and the cycle of the year. And all of this encourages her association with Anubis.

Hekate, 6th century BCE.

As Egyptian gods and goddesses became popular in Greece and Rome, Anubis was often invoked alongside Hekate during spell work, especially for spells involving banishment, protection, or cursing. Both Hekate and Anubis were represented by black dogs, and spell work involving depictions of dogs were common to both. Today, both are associated with witchcraft and the occult and both hold the title Keeper of Keys, *Kleidoukhos*, referring to their roles as gatekeepers to the Underworld and masters of the secrets and mysteries of life, death, and the occult.

In my own practice, I work with both Anubis and Hekate, individually and together. I have come to see Hekate as my "witch mother," with whom I work to learn more about practicing witchcraft. Anubis has become more the patron deity to whom I am dedicated. Although I very rarely use that term in reference to him, it does describe my relationship with him. I work closely with him in both shadow work and in any spell work or magick involving inner journeys.

Anubis and the Sun

Anubis, in his role as Hermanubis, was often portrayed with a solar disc on his head, situated between his ears. This was likely a sign of his status and importance, as many gods who wore these disks were associated with the role of kingship in some way. It was also a symbol of divinity and power. Moreover, when you consider that Hermanubis may possibly be a combination of Horus and Anubis, it makes sense to see him depicted with a solar disc, as Horus was closely tied to the sun. Many modern artworks depict Anubis with the sun in some capacity.

Anubis is also sometimes referred to as the son of Ra, the god of the sun, giving him another connection to solar energies. In one instance in the *Greek Magical Papyri* (PGM IV, 94–153), Anubis declares that he holds the crown of Ra, with the solar disc, and he intends to give it to his father, Osiris. This doesn't necessarily mean that Anubis had it as his own to wear, but it does show that he holds the power to grant kingship, status, and energies associated with the sun.

Anubis and the Moon

Typically, the moon was associated with Khonsu, god of the moon, portrayed as a young man with the head of a falcon and a lunar disc on his head. The moon was also tied to one of Horus's eyes (the other being associated with the sun). Moreover, Horus was the falcon-headed god of kingship, light, healing, and the sky.

The moon also represents the cycles of life and death, and this is the key to understanding this particular depiction of Anubis. The moon goes through its cycle every twenty-nine days, beginning with the New Moon, waxing until full, and waning again until it disappears from the night sky. Then it is reborn as another New Moon. Thus, every twenty-nine days, it cycles symbolically through birth, life, death, and rebirth. There are a few instances in the history of ancient Egypt, and even Rome, in which Anubis was portrayed bent over and holding a lunar disc in front of another figure, as if offering that person the keys to the cycle of rebirth upon death. In one depiction, the lunar disc is presented to one of Egypt's most famous queens, Hatshepsut, during her birth in order to help her ascend to divinity and ensure her longevity and success in life and the afterlife. Here again, Anubis holds the key to granting power, kingship, and status while ensuring rebirth.

Anubis and the Stars

Egyptian astronomy was an enormously important blending of science and magick. Significantly, the constellation we know today as Ursa Minor (Little Bear) was associated in ancient Egypt with the jackal. This constellation includes Polaris, or the North Star. When depicting the night sky in artwork and reliefs, the Egyptians often put the jackal constellation in the very center of the map of the night sky, where he could act as a guide for those lost in the darkness—a perfect symbolism for Anubis.

Sirius, the Dog Star, is associated with many deities, including Anubis. This is the brightest star in the night sky, shining brighter than any other star (not including visible planets). In fact, the name Sirius refers to how bright and glowing it is. But the term "Dog Star" comes from the fact that it's part of the constellation Canis Major (Great Dog). Sirius was an important star in ancient Egypt, as it marked the beginning of the new year as it rose above the horizon. Because of this, and because of its brightness, it makes sense to associate this star with the "light in the darkness," as well as with being able to find your way through the darkness—with Anubis.

Anubis and Saint Christopher

Saint Christopher is a Christian saint who eventually became loosely associated with Anubis. Christopher was the patron saint of travelers. (Reminds me of a psychopomp!) He was also a healer who protected travelers from bad weather and storms. (Sound familiar?) He was initially depicted as a man with the head of a dog wearing either robes or a warrior's armor, with a red cape and holding a spear. He was sometimes referred to as one of the *cynocephali,* or "dog-headed," and depictions of him as such have been found across the Middle East and even in Europe.

One famous story involving Saint Christopher tells how he carried a child across a body of water. The child became increasingly heavy and, by the time he reached the shore, he realized that the child had grown into Christ. Christ then admitted who he was, although Christopher was doubtful at first. In order to prove himself, Christ ordered Saint Christopher to put his staff into the ground. When he did, it grew into a palm tree, recalling depictions of Hermanubis holding a palm leaf.

This story also highlights a connection between Anubis and Saint Christopher in their roles as guide, or psychopomp. Just as Anubis ushered the souls of the deceased into the afterlife, Saint Christopher ushered the child across the water. Some historians have even drawn analogies between this story and the idea of transformation that is associated with Anubis. Yet others, instead of arguing for this connection, speculate that it could have resulted from a misinterpretation of the word *Canaanite* (someone from the land of Canaan) and the Latin term *canineus,* meaning "doglike."

Of course, today we can't know exactly why Saint Christopher was depicted in the way he was. Was it intentional? Was it a subtle way to bring Hermanubis into the era of the new religion? Or was it simply a mistake? We'll never know for sure, but it seems to me that there is a definite argument to be made for the association of Saint Christopher with Anubis, not just based in appearance, but in areas of influence and roles.

In case you are wondering what ever happened to Saint Christopher, one legend suggests that he was forced to serve in the Roman army and was eventually martyred in Syria for refusing to change his religious beliefs.

The Cult of Anubis

After his entry into Greece and Rome via Hermanubis, Anubis's following continued to grow and expand, just as Isis's did. There were depictions of him and examples of groups dedicated to him well into the 2nd century CE.

Anubis was included in spell work alongside Hermes, Hekate, and other chthonic gods and goddesses. These spells were typically classified as "necromancy," but this isn't the classic necromancy that you may be thinking of from popular movies, TV shows, and video games. We aren't talking here about raising the dead. These spells could include anything from erotic and love spells to spells for prophetic dreams, curses and banishments, protection, and even invisibility spells. Though some were dark and intended to grant influence over someone else, many were simply spells for protection and vision. Anubis was also petitioned for divination, visions, and prophetic dreams, as seen in the *Greek Magical Papyri*, as well as for connecting with departed loved ones and communicating with them.

If you are interested in exploring occult practices, Anubis can act as a guide. Just be aware that reaching into the world of spirits isn't always going to give you something fluffy and pretty. The world isn't always love and light. There are energies that are dangerous and chaotic. There are darker forces at play in the world, and many stories tell of the pain, loss, and suffering of those who misuse them. If you plan to delve into any kind of witchcraft or occult practices, I strongly urge you to study and learn before jumping into anything.

The "Modern" Anubis

Anubis has somehow remained relevant across time, across cultures, and across distances. Over thousands of years—from the far-off sands of ancient Egypt to modern-day cities across every continent—Anubis persists. He is the quiet shadow that rests in the corner, waiting for us to happen upon him. We recognize him and his role, even without knowing anything about him. We recognize his name and know who he is, proving in a sense that death, itself, never dies.

Anubis is the ultimate liminal deity—one who stands in the between spaces. He is a part of a great circle that encompasses light and darkness, the four corners of heaven and earth, and the four elements. No matter how you interpret his origin myths, he is born of two realms—either the sky and earth (Ra and Hesat) or this world and the Underworld (Nephthys and Osiris). He is associated with the sun and the moon, and the winter and summer solstices. Dawn and dusk are sacred to him, as are the equinoxes, which balance light and darkness. He exists as a being of both life and death, in both the celestial realm and the regions of death.

Anubis has influence over magick, divination, seers, and occult seekers. His reach is expansive; he is far more than a deity of death and embalming. He is Great Shaman, Master of Mysteries, Keeper of Keys, and Opener of Ways.

In Part II, we'll examine practical ways in which you can begin to build a relationship with this complex god. As you move through the following chapters, I encourage you to consider all the various ways in which you can connect with his many aspects. Think about them, meditate on them, and remember to record your thoughts in your journal.

Prayer to the Great Protector

Dua Anpu, Great Protector
Whose gaze is ever watchful,
Keep an eye out for those with malign intent.
Protect me from them.
Shroud me in your cloak of darkness
That I may be unseen.
Protect me with your obsidian shield,
Strong and impenetrable.

Journal Prompts

- Which of these "other" aspects of Anubis do you find the most interesting?

- How does the liminality of Anubis speak to you today?

Part Two

WORKING WITH ANUBIS

Part Two

WORKING WITH
ANUBIS

CHAPTER 10

Signs and Messages

"Find me in the shadows. Seek me in the light. I am within and without.
I rest in the in-between spaces. I am the whisper in the night.
I am the light within the darkness."

ANUBIS TO ME DURING A MEDITATION

think the question that I get asked more than any other is: "How do I know if Anubis is calling me?" Signs and messages from the spirit world are highly personal. The signs that the gods and spirits send me may or may not be the same ones they send you. Chances are, if you've read through Part I, you already know that.

Signs can be physical, coming through animals, symbols, words and phrases, objects, songs, or patterns that are relevant to you, your life, your question, or your situation. They can also be intangible, rooted in feelings and sensations—a song in your head, visions, dreams, intuitive feelings, or thoughts that seem to appear randomly or that may not quite seem to be your own. They can come in the form of a friend who calls to say something that is eerily relevant in the moment. Some of the signs I've either received myself or heard about from others include symbols like ankhs, pyramids, bones, skulls, the Eye of Horus, gravestones, scales, and the sun and moon together. Animals like dogs, jackals, wolves, coyotes, foxes, and leopards may also carry a message, as can relevant colors like black and gold, or brown, white, or gray. Dreams about death and dying, loss, journeys or winding pathways, unlocking doors, keys and portals, representations of balance (light/dark, sun/moon, etc.) can contain important messages.

The thing about signs, however, is that you have to *recognize* them in order to learn from them.

Recognizing Signs

There have been a number of articles, and even whole books, written on how to identify when something is a sign and when it's just a mundane occurrence. Learning to recognize signs can be tricky, but my advice is simply to go with your gut. It's incredibly easy to overthink this and get lost in trying to figure out whether something is or is not a sign. Signs quite often just *stand out*. An animal that is really out of place at a particular moment or behaves in a peculiar way could be a sign. A song that comes on at just the right moment you need to hear it or an ad that seems eerily relevant could be signs. Trust your intuition. And don't be overly analytical—easier said than done, I know.

Sometimes, however, a dog is just a dog. Sometimes what you think is a sign doesn't mean anything profound. And while that can be disappointing, it's the reality. Dogs are pretty commonplace to see while out and about, for example. When you are uncertain whether something is a sign or not, ask yourself what you felt in the moment. Did what you saw make you stop? Did it get your attention? Did you feel anything in particular at that moment? Did it connect with something that's going on in your life right now?

Let's say, for example, that you're trying to figure out whether you should move to a new apartment. Where you're living now is so expensive that it's forcing you to live paycheck to paycheck. You found a cheaper place that could save you a lot of money, but moving means that you will be farther from work. You are trying to decide whether this would be a good decision or not, so you ask for a sign from the universe. Later that day, you are out grocery shopping when you hear *Hit the Road Jack* being played in the store. Now, that's a song you don't hear played very often. So, to me, that might likely be a sign, because it stands out from the normal course of things and is just a little too "spot on" to be just a coincidence.

Of course, it's probably never a good idea to make huge life decisions based solely on signs. A sign can certainly act as confirmation, but there's also power in logic and thinking things through thoroughly. For me, I believe in a balanced approach. Often signs either confirm something that I already knew and needed to remember, or they may be the "final push" I need to get off the fence. However signs materialize for you, please don't make rash decisions based on them alone. And as you read through this chapter and begin to become more comfortable recognizing signs, keep in mind that what I give you here are my experiences; they may not necessarily be the same as yours or anyone else's.

Remember as well that Anubis is often a silent Watcher. Sometimes you may ask him for a sign and receive nothing. That doesn't mean he doesn't care. It just means that he has a different approach. In my experience, he likes to let you figure things out for yourself. And he's also Master of Mysteries, so when he does send a sign, it may arrive quietly and unannounced, sometimes when you're least expecting it. Unfortunately, that can make it even harder to determine what's a sign and what's not.

Messages from Anubis

It took me quite awhile to realize that I rarely get physical signs from Anubis, although I sometimes do. When I've worked with other deities, like Hekate, I've gotten a lot of clear physical or audible signs. In fact, Hekate likes to send me *actual* signs as signs—weird license plates, strangely relevant billboards and street signs, and random words that appear entirely out of place but somehow fit my circumstance.

Anubis, on the other hand, is a little more subtle. Sometimes he doesn't send me anything—perhaps because he wants me to figure things out on my own. When I do receive a sign from him, however, it's usually quite distinct. My first encounter with him involved the run-in with canines I had as a child. Now, the signs that I receive from him seem to be closely tied to trusting my intuition and letting it guide me, rather than expecting to see a sign every time I turn the corner.

So how does Anubis communicate with me? I've learned that I can best be open to receiving messages from him when my mind is quiet. In those moments when you are more relaxed and your brain isn't full of thoughts buzzing around, your psychic senses can be more alert and receptive to communication. For some, this happens during meditation; for others, including myself, it can happen when I'm walking, or driving, or performing some mundane task. I often hear an inner voice or have a relevant thought pop up while I'm on a walk. Sometimes a song runs unbidden through my head; sometimes I hear the whisper of a word or phrase on the wind.

I frequently experience visions of Anubis during meditation, as you can see from the epigraphs that introduce some of these chapters. I find that he would rather I come to him before he gives me the information that I need to know. In chapter 11, you'll find a meditation exercise that will take you on a journey to meet Anubis. Try it and see how he responds.

One of the most startling times that Anubis appeared to me was during an experience I had while I was showering. For me, taking a shower is a very calming, relaxing experience in which I can unwind and let loose the thoughts that are crowding my busy mind. When our minds are clearest, that's when we are more open to receiving messages and visions. And so there he was. With me in the shower. Not creepily, just communicating with me when my mind was most receptive that day.

But the most powerful way in which I know he's nearby is by *feeling*. By sensing his energy. Maybe it's just that I know he's around. Maybe it's an actual experience of his energy. Maybe it's a little of both. I had two people ask me recently (around the same time, oddly enough; a sign, perhaps?) what Anubis's energy feels like to me. The only way I could explain it was to say that it feels like a strong, solid, grounded, protective, yet also calming energy that I sense in my core.

Answering Anubis

I can't tell you what Anubis wants from you. That is a very personal matter between you and him. For me, he wants to lead me through a life of challenges—turmoil, transitions, changes, and chaos—so I can come out on the other side with my head held high. And he wants me to use these experiences to make a difference in my life and, hopefully, in the lives of others. He also wants to guide me down a spiritual path that has forever changed my life.

When you receive a sign from Anubis, try reaching out to him in return, once you feel comfortable doing so. The chapters that follow will show you some practical ways in which you can connect with him and begin to build communication with him. In them, you'll find suggestions for building a daily practice that can deepen your relationship and help you "get to know him,"' so to speak. We'll also explore offerings, rituals, spell work, and celebrations appropriate for working with this complex deity.

Remember to keep a journal of the things you see, hear, feel, and discover as you go through these experiences. Keep a record of the signs, the messages, the visions, the dreams, or even the feelings and sensations that you have. Return to them later so you can explore their deeper meaning. Keep track of them over time and see how they develop. Try to identify patterns that may have special significance. And most important of all—enjoy the journey, knowing with certainty that Anubis will protect you and guide you on your way.

Prayer to Call Back Power

Hail to Anubis, Sovereign of Death and Lord of the Underworld!
You stand in the liminal space between life and death,
Master of your Realms, answering to none.
Be with me in this space
As I call back my power from all persons, all spaces, and all things.
In all directions of time and across all planes of existence,
May it be my own.
Protect me and guard me that I may keep it.
For I am the Sovereign of my life.

Journal Prompts

- Are there any events, experiences, or signs in your life that, in retrospect, you think may have been sent by Anubis? What were they?

- If not, what signs and associations speak to you the most?

CHAPTER 11

Communicating with Anubis

Words are a pretext. It is the inner bond that draws
one person to another, not words.

RUMI

Now that you've come to understand a little more about who Anubis is and how he can help you in your life, you may be wondering how you can communicate with him. There are several ways to approach Anubis—some formal and some informal—and there is not necessarily a "right" or "wrong" way to establish communication with him. But there are some that may work better for you than others. In this chapter, we'll discuss a few ways to communicate with him and consider when they might be useful.

Again, there isn't necessarily a right or wrong way to communicate with Anubis (or with any deity, in my opinion). It really depends on the situation and your own preferences. Before we go any further, however, I want to point out a few very important things to remember when reaching out to any deity.

1.   Respect, respect, respect. Never, ever approach deities in a disrespectful way. You will regret it. Even if you are angry or

frustrated, be mindful of how you speak to them and the energy that you bring. Speak the truth, if you wish, but do so in a manner that is respectful. No one wants to anger a god.

2. Never demand anything of deities. They are not required to come at your beck and call or do your bidding. The gods are not here to serve you.

3. Don't make promises you won't keep. There may be consequences for breaking a promise to a god.

4. Start with a clear mind, or as clear a mind as you can. This is something I've learned through my own experience.

5. Be mindful of your surroundings. Be sure that you're safe.

6. Don't get discouraged if you get nothing in response. The gods may be silent, but that does not mean they are ignoring you or that they don't care. And it definitely does not mean that you "did it wrong." It's just that the gods have their own agendas and their own paths to travel.

7. Trust that the gods are listening, although they may not always respond in the time that you expect them to. Time works differently for them. Moreover, they may have a particular reason for not giving you the answers you seek right away. It may be that you have a lesson to learn.

And remember, Anubis can have a strong, grounding, protective energy that can fill a room, but he can also be subtle and rather quiet at times. There's a reason he is called Master of Mysteries! You will not always feel him as a dominant presence that fills the space. In fact, it may seem as if he isn't there at all. He may simply be resting in the shadows, ever watchful.

Meditation

Meditation can be a powerful tool for connecting with any deity, spirit, or entity—and this is true for Anubis as well. Starting from the point of a quiet mind can help you to establish a clear point of connection with him. There are many types of meditation, each meant to achieve a different purpose. You can do a seated meditation like the one at the end of this chapter, or use controlled breathing practices, or take a walk in a quiet place, or simply step away from the business of your day for a few moments—whatever works best for you. Meditation isn't always about attempting to empty your mind. At least not my meditation.

My most frequent form of meditation is simply walking in a quiet place—preferably in nature. You'll find an example of this kind of meditation at the end of the next chapter. I find this helps me to clear my mind so I can commune with Anubis and simply be in his presence. But I also sometimes do a walking meditation when I want to ponder the mysteries of the universe, or something similar. Sometimes I even find myself speaking to Anubis as I walk. This is a powerful experience, but the key for me is that it helps me to quiet my busy mind.

Journeying

A deeper kind of meditative exercise that I enjoy is journeying. Journeying involves a great deal of visualization, which may not come naturally to everyone. It may take some time and practice to build this skill, but it can be an incredibly profound way to connect with Anubis, because it really utilizes all of your psychic senses.

When journeying, I enter into a meditative space in which my spirit can meet Anubis. Sometimes we meet in my ethereal sacred space (see chapter 14), and sometimes we meet in a location that I don't always know until I am there. I just let my spirit take me to wherever it needs to go, or wherever Anubis leads me. There, I can ask him questions that are on my mind. Sometimes I ask him for a particular favor, like protection. At other times, I simply wish to commune with him, to be in his presence and let come to me what may.

Before you begin any kind of journey, there are a few extremely important things to keep in mind. Taking a few moments to establish a few key conditions will make the experience go more smoothly and also help ensure the overall safety and well-being of your physical body, as well as your spirit.

1. Be sure that you are always in a safe location—ideally, at home.

2. If there are others around, be sure they are people you trust.

3. Make sure you find a place where you won't be disturbed. This may be difficult, but it's important, as any distractions or noise can keep you from entering or staying in a meditative state. So try to do this when you're alone. Turn off notifications on your phone. Turn off the TV. You may find that soft music helps set the space, or you may wish to have complete silence. That's up to you.

4. Be sure that you are comfortable—seated in a comfortable chair or lying down. Wear loose comfortable clothing that won't be distracting while you are journeying.

5. Keep water and a snack on hand for when you finish.

Conversation

I don't know if it's because I have worked with Anubis for so long that I have become comfortable speaking with him openly and honestly, or if I am just bold, but I have what I like to call "conversations" with Anubis. These are not like conventional conversations between two people. He isn't standing in front of me in a physical body, interacting with me, and using body language and gestures. He isn't on the other end of a phone call. He isn't on a video chat with me—although I have always thought that would be a fun, modern approach to connecting with him. My conversations with Anubis consist mostly of me speaking to him directly.

I sometimes do this while I am on one of my meditation walks. Of course, when I do, I have to remain mindful of my surroundings, so I don't necessarily always speak out loud. As much as I don't care what other people think of me most of the time, I don't want to draw unnecessary attention to myself. Sometimes I have these conversations while I'm in the shower or while driving. I find I can speak to Anubis when everything else in my world has fallen away and I have the opportunity to quiet my mind or to think deeply. Sometimes I converse with him while I am sitting at his altar space in my home (see chapter 14). It really depends on the situation and when I feel the urge or need.

I am very attuned to the spirit world and to my deities. Because of this, I have to protect my own space and energy. I cannot remain open to being approached 100 percent of the time, so I generally have to set aside specific times and places to connect to other deities and spirits. But, for me, with Anubis it's different.

Do I always get a response from him? No. Sometimes I am met with complete silence. I used to wonder if he even heard me or if he cared. But I now know that he does hear me and he always cares. I understand that deities have their own lives and agendas, and that I am not the only practitioner approaching them. That doesn't mean that they care more for one person than another. It just means that they may simply not wish to respond 100 percent of the time. And that's their prerogative.

Prayer

Prayer can be a good way to connect with a deity. I know that some witches and Pagans cringe when they hear the word "prayer." For some, it brings up strong associations with other religions and traditions with which they may have had negative experiences in the past. And some tend to avoid it because it may not feel like territory that they can even approach. That is understandable, and if that is true for you, there are certainly other ways to approach the gods. But I can assure you that humans were praying long before established religions took up the practice and people from all faiths around the world pray. Prayer is not exclusive to one particular tradition, nor does it *belong* to one particular religion. Prayer is available to all.

As we have seen, in ancient Egypt, people prayed to Anubis for protection and guidance in the afterlife. They called out to him in cemeteries and places where embalming rituals were performed, asking that he cast his watchful gaze on those who had passed on. Embalmers prayed to him to guide their hands as they worked the sacred ceremonies to prepare the deceased for the afterlife.

Prayer can be used for a variety of purposes. You can pray when you want something, calling to spirits or deities in the hope that they will respond by granting you a favor or a boon. You can pray out of gratitude, offering your thanks to the deity or spirit you are addressing.

You can also pray for healing, guidance, love, or wisdom—the list goes on and on.

Prayer can be either formal or informal, depending on the situation. Some like to speak from the heart in the moment, so they simply pour out what is on their minds. Others write down prayers in advance so they know exactly what they want to say, especially if the prayer is being said in preparation for a special occasion or event.

I pray to Anubis on a daily basis; it is part of my daily devotional practice. Whether or not you want to make your prayers formal is entirely up to you. From my own experience over the many years I have worked with Anubis, I know that he does not expect or require that. In fact, I have had some of my best connections with him simply by speaking freely, openly, and honestly. Coming to him from a place of authenticity and sincerity can be extremely powerful. When I pray to him informally, however, I always make sure that I clearly state an intended purpose and specific outcome—praying for protection, for example.

If you prefer, you can certainly prepare what you want to say ahead of time, whether your prayer itself is formal or not. Meeting a deity for the first time can be intimidating. So you may be more comfortable writing down what you want to say in advance. Make it as formal or as informal as you like. Just be sure that your prayer is coming from a place of sincerity and authenticity. Throughout this book, I have given you prayers and chants that you can use to petition Anubis for a variety of purposes. Use them to reach out to him or—even better—write your own.

Divination

Anubis, as Master of Mysteries, is an excellent deity to call on during any kind of divinatory work. Divination is a spiritual practice that has been used for thousands of years. Across time and cultures, people have sought wisdom and guidance from the gods from oracles, seers, shamans, priests, and witches for just about everything—life goals, aspirations, marriage, births and children, decision-making, and more. Tarot cards and oracle cards, for example, can be a good way to connect with Anubis in a daily devotional practice. They let you ask questions and receive answers that can help you navigate through troubling times in your life. Many tarot readers and mediums use a guide during their sessions as a means of protection and of connecting to a higher energy. Some ask a particular deity for a message. Anubis can act as both medium and guide.

Tarot and oracle decks differ slightly. Tarot decks contain a specific number of cards divided into the Major and Minor Arcana. The Major Arcana represent broad archetypes found throughout life, and often indicate people or big-picture themes. The Minor Arcana are divided by number and suits that are often associated with the elements. They focus on smaller, more specific aspects of life. Tarot readings are based on the meaning of these cards, as well as the visual imagery they contain and the reader's own intuition.

Oracle cards, on the other hand, focus on a specific deck-wide theme. They can contain any number of cards, but the number is often significant in some way. Each card carries a specific meaning that fits within the theme of the deck. Oracle decks tend to be good for beginners, but I highly recommend learning at least something about the tarot. Start with books specifically geared to beginners, like those by Theresa Reed or Rachel Pollack. There are also many good books out there that go into greater depth about how to do tarot readings and incorporate them into your daily life.

Over the years, I have found that there are some tarot cards that are specifically connected to Anubis—cards like Death, Judgment, Strength, the King of Swords, and even sometimes the Tower, because chaos and change ultimately lead to transformation. You may discover that he appears to you in other cards.

There are several decks that I recommend for use with Anubis. These include:

- *Anubis Oracle: A Journey into the Shamanic Mysteries of Egypt* by Nicki Scully and Linda Star Wolf (Bear & Company, 2008)

- *Egyptian Tarot Deck* by Lo Scarabeo (Llewellyn, 2000)

- *Egyptian Gods Oracle Deck* by Silvana Alasia (Llewellyn, 2022)

- *Wild Unknown Tarot Deck* by Kim Krans (HarperOne, 2016)

- *Weiser Tarot* by Arthur Waite, Pamela Smith, and the Editors of Weiser Books (Weiser, 2022)

The tarot Judgment card, one often associated with Anubis.

Receiving Answers

Waiting to see if you receive an answer from a deity can be frustrating, but the important thing to remember is that the gods are beings with their own will and desires who work on their own schedules. Sometimes Anubis does "answer" me, although often in the form of a sign or message that I may not immediately understand. I can't tell you what these signs or messages will be, as they are highly personal. But I can tell you what they've been for me and share my experiences understanding them with you.

For me, synchronicities are the most common messages I get from Anubis. Synchronicities are those little moments when something happens that you can't explain. They can come in the form of physical, tangible things that you encounter that feel special and relevant to you, to your life, or to a situation at hand. These signs can include animals, objects, symbols, words or phrases, numbers, a tarot card, even a person—anything relevant to your life or the question at hand that seems significant or out of the ordinary. Some of the signs that people associate with Anubis are the ankh and canines—jackals, wolves, dogs, coyotes, foxes. A dog that stands out and seems to be more than just an ordinary dog, for example. Perhaps you spot an animal that seems peculiar, rare, or out of place. Perhaps you see a random billboard or a sign on a building. Perhaps someone says something to you that just stands out. It could be just about anything. I have learned to be attentive to all these kinds of signs.

Music is a hugely important part of my life. So sometimes I receive a sign or message from Anubis through a random song I hear on the radio or when a relevant song just pops into my head. Songs pop into my head all the time, sometimes because the radio overplays them, sometimes because they relate to something that I'm obsessing over, sometimes because I have played them over and over. But sometimes it's more than that. The songs that often mean something for me are those that either come to me completely out of the blue or that are playing in my mind when I wake up. When this occurs, it's usually a song I haven't heard in a long time, yet its relevance is oddly fitting for the situation at hand.

Build a communication channel with Anubis and listen for the messages you get in response. As your practice deepens, integrate more elements into it—like offerings and rituals. The more you do, the stronger the relationship you build with him will be.

Journey to Meet Anubis

I highly recommend this practice as a way to deepen your relationship with Anubis and gain access to the knowledge, resources, and experiences that you need along your spiritual path. Wherever this journey takes you, it will bring you into closer connection with him.

Before you begin, fill a glass with water and prepare a light snack for yourself. Place them somewhere where they will be handy when you return from your journey.

Sit comfortably in a chair, with your feet flat on the floor. Take a few moments to settle into the chair, letting yourself become comfortable and fully relaxed. Take three deep breaths, filling your lungs with air and pulling it down to your diaphragm. Close your eyes, then take three more deep breaths and let your body settle even more.

Imagine there are roots growing downward through your legs and out from the bottoms of your feet into the ground beneath you. Feel them reach deep into the earth, grounding your body into the space. Imagine there are branches emerging from the top of your head and reaching up into the sky, connecting with the energy of the sun, the moon, and the stars. Let that energy uplift you. Then imagine that the roots below you and the branches above you meet in your body and intertwine at your core.

Take a few more deep breaths and rest for a moment in this in-between space. Let yourself sink into a meditative state. Feel yourself sinking deeper, your soul almost freeing itself from your body. With each breath, you feel more and more weightless and free. You are completely rested within this space.

Imagine there is a door in front of you. You immediately recognize that this door is meant just for you. Pause a moment to inspect it. What does it look like? Is it rectangular or rounded at the top? What color is it? What does the knob look like? Does it have any ornaments or decorations? Make a mental note of these details, then reach for the handle. Turn it and push the door open.

As you walk through the door, you find yourself in a long dark corridor. You have trouble seeing at first, but there are torches lining the wall and your eyes adjust quickly. You see that the walls are made of sand-colored stone blocks that feel smooth and cold to the touch. The floor is the same color. The brackets that hold the torches are gold, decorated with turquoise and ruby stones.

A faint whisper in the air calls you to move forward, and you begin walking down the corridor. After walking for what seems like a long while, you finally come to a second door. This door is large, made of dark-colored wood with golden hinges and handle. There are swirling patterns carved into it with a large ankh in the center. In the center of the loop of the ankh there is a black obsidian stone. You feel called to open the door, so you do.

On the other side is a large, expansive field overhung with clouds. It's not quite nighttime—perhaps either dawn or dusk—but a faint light illuminates the scene enough for you to see. You look around and see stretches of tall grass with flecks of dark trees here and there. Patches of blue and purple flowers seem almost to glow in the dark. You take a deep breath and smell the scent of wood, but also of cinnamon and sage.

Your attention is drawn to a nearby circle of stones with a pedestal in the center. On the pedestal is a single black candle in a golden holder that is decorated with the same turquoise and ruby stones you saw in the torches moments ago. There is a match next to it. Instinctively, you know what to do. You strike the match and gently light the candle. Then you extinguish the match and put it back on the pedestal.

You hear a rustling nearby and turn to see a figure approaching. It's Anubis. He is quite tall. You feel a little intimidated at first, but that quickly subsides as he smiles at you. You stop to gaze at him. What does he look like? Does he have a human form? Is he jackal-headed? What else do you notice? What is he wearing? What color is his clothing? Is he wearing any adornments or jewelry?

You notice that he holds a small, golden ankh in his hand. With his other hand, he motions gently for you to come closer. You approach him, and he smiles again. He has an important message for you. He begins to speak. What does he say to you? Listen carefully to what he tells you and remember the details for later.

Now is the time to ask him any questions on your mind. What do you want to know?

When you feel that your meeting is over, you thank Anubis and turn toward the door through which you came. Before you leave, you turn. Anubis raises his hand in farewell before disappearing. You extinguish the candle and take a deep breath before heading back down the corridor. As you walk, you recall the words he spoke to you. You pass through your personal door at the end of the corridor and close it behind you.

Pause for a moment. Take several deep breaths. With each breath, let yourself become aware of your body and your surroundings. Wiggle your fingers and your toes. Move your head. Begin to stretch a little. And finally, open your eyes.

Drink some water and eat the snack that you prepared, fully returning yourself back into your physical body. In your journal, write down what you remember, including as many details as you can and paying close attention to what Anubis told you. Record as much of what he said as you can remember.

Journal Prompts

- Which of these spiritual practices do you already use in your daily practice?

- What method of communicating with Anubis are you most interested in trying?

CHAPTER 12

Building a Daily Devotional Practice

*However difficult life may seem, there is always something
you can do and succeed at.*

STEPHEN HAWKING

Over the years, on various online platforms, I have gotten a lot of
questions from people who want to know what to do once they
have received some kind of message or communication from a deity. In
this case, we are talking about Anubis, of course, but many of the ideas I
am going to discuss here can be applied to any deity.

People often tell me that they have gotten some kind of recognizable
sign from Anubis, perhaps one that I mentioned in chapter 10. Perhaps
they have developed an inexplicable interest in learning more about him
that was not there before (intuition at its finest!). Or perhaps they just
feel an innate curiosity about connecting with him. Their next question is
usually: "Now what?" Of course, this is usually followed by more questions, like: "How can I connect to Anubis?" or "How do I even begin
to deepen a relationship with Anubis?" And this leads us to the more
general question of what it even means to embark on a "relationship"
with a deity.

Think of the people who are important to you in life—your closest friends, for instance. I assume that getting to know them did not happen overnight. You probably spent months, years, maybe even decades spending time with them, talking to them, and learning about who they are, where they came from, and what they like. Eventually, you began to understand the details and the intricacies of who they are as people and how they think about the world. You probably spent countless hours getting to know them.

With the caveat that deities are vastly different from humans and far more complex than we can ever begin to comprehend, you can say the same thing about building a relationship with the gods and goddesses. You have to spend time getting to know them. You have to spend time *with* them, in their presence, to really deepen that relationship and take it to the next level. Essentially, you have to build that connection and deepen your understanding of who they are. You have to develop a relationship that will grow over time. And that's where a daily devotional practice comes in.

A daily devotional practice is essentially the time that you spend every single day doing something that is spiritually meaningful to you. This does not have to consist of grand gestures, nor does it have to take up a lot of time. We are all busy and have other commitments in our lives. But it is important to find a time, even if it is just fifteen minutes, when you can commit to doing something for your spiritual health. Some do a tarot reading for their day. Others read, meditate, listen to music, pray, or perform some other activity. What's important is that you build this practice into your day so that it becomes a routine rather than a chore.

Daily Rituals

Think of your daily rituals—your daily routine. For me, I wake up and turn off my alarm. Then I get out of bed and freshen up in the bathroom. Then I head to the kitchen and get myself coffee and either yogurt or oatmeal (my go-to breakfast). And then the magickal part of my day begins—my daily devotional practice. I will talk more about that in a minute. The rest of my day includes working from home most days, going for a walk in the park after work, returning home to cook dinner, and then spending the evening doing something that brings me joy—reading, writing, journaling, watching a good TV show, or playing video games. Before bed, I like to make sure the kitchen is clean and ready for the next day. I put my dishes in the dishwasher, get my coffee ready to make in the morning, and quickly clean up. Then I brush my teeth and get ready for bed. Before bed, I like to do something mindful like meditation or reading before I fall asleep.

My point in listing all this is that all of these tasks and chores have become routine for me. They are all things that I do every day, or nearly every day. They are not necessarily activities that I need to plan for or set reminders to remember.

Was it always that way? No. All routines and habits take time to establish. And the exact same process is required to build a daily devotional practice. It may take time to figure out what you want to do for your daily routine, and it may take some trial and error to decide what works best for you. A daily practice does not necessarily have to be devotional. We are not talking about becoming some kind of monk or priest, although the role of priesthood in devotion to a deity is something that some feel called to pursue. But that kind of dedication is different from the kind of daily practice I'm talking about. What I'm describing here can consist of a devotion to healing, or working on a specific practice or field of study, or connecting with the elements, or anything that is meaningful enough to you that you want to dedicate time and energy to it each day. In this chapter, we'll focus on what it means to build a daily practice in devotion to a specific deity—in this case, Anubis.

Ritual statue of Anubis.

Making a spiritual practice a part of your daily routine is a way to honor the gods and goddesses to whom you feel closest. In essence, you are devoting yourself to deepening your connection with them and to building a relationship with them. For me personally, this gives me something to look forward to each day. I look forward to those morning hours when I commune with the deities and spirits. Why would you do this? Because it honors them and gives thanks for their presence in your life, whatever that may look like. It gives you a sense of purpose and direction as you go through your day. It also strengthens your relationship with them.

Building a relationship with a deity is not a one-way street, however. Gods and goddesses are not pawns who come when beckoned. They are independent, sovereign beings with their own ideas, desires, and goals. Their time is just as valuable as yours, and you are not the only practitioner who is approaching them. Asking something of them requires giving something in return. You cannot expect them simply to come when called and do whatever you ask (or demand) of them. They are not your personal, exclusive servants. It simply does not work that way.

You may be thinking that you are so busy that you don't know whether you have the time to commit to a daily devotional practice—and that's certainly understandable. If that's the case, try devoting just fifteen minutes a day and see how that works out. There is value in devoting whatever amount of time you can spare in your day to your spiritual growth. The benefits include building and deepening your relationship with your chosen deity, and gaining a deeper sense of connection and purpose. You may find that a daily practice brings you a sense of satisfaction and purpose. You may find yourself feeling calmer and more at peace.

Before You Begin

There are four key things to remember that can help you build and maintain a daily devotional practice: *Be realistic. Stick with it. Schedule wisely. And make it personal.*

You may have the urge (or perhaps not) to jump in and commit yourself to doing a number of different things every day. But that may not be realistic for you. We all have other things going on in our lives, so it may not be possible to sit down and go through an extensive list of activities as a daily practice. Pick one practice to start with—meditation, prayer, chanting, writing, reading, drumming, dancing, singing, crafting, or simply enjoying a mindful moment in the morning. Whatever speaks to you most strongly, do that.

Start with something you know you will be comfortable doing regularly. It is better to pick something that you know you will do each day than to try to do whatever you feel like each day. Of course, you can add things, remove things, and change things up. Personally, I have found that my daily practice shifts and changes over time, depending on my life circumstances, my own personal needs, and my own physical and mental energy levels. Just be sure that, whatever you choose to do, you make the commitment to continue doing it for as long as you and your deity have agreed.

The second key is to stick with it! Neglecting a daily practice that you have promised to perform can have consequences. For me, I end up with broken statues. I know that sounds odd, and perhaps a little "woowoo," but each time in my life that I have neglected to keep my promises to Anubis, I have ended up with one of my statues of him either partially broken or completely shattered. They have mysteriously fallen off shelves or tables where they were sitting while not a single soul was around. Nor were there any pets nearby or any windows open. I woke up one morning to find a small figure of Anubis on the floor with his head broken off and a chip in his tail.

In my early thirties, I decided to make a huge change in my life by moving from the Midwest, where I had lived my whole life, to the West Coast, where I have resided ever since. When I arrived after a long journey in the middle of winter, I found that nothing had been broken on the trip—except a small statue of Anubis. And then I realized I had neglected my daily devotional practice on the trip and broken promises I had made to him. The broken statue was a clear message to me that I was not fulfilling my end of the bargain. So be sure to find a way to hold yourself accountable to the commitments you make. Without some sort of accountability, they are just empty words.

The third key is to pick a time of day that you know will fit into your schedule. For me, that time is first thing in the morning. I like to get up early. I wish I were a night owl who could stay up late and enjoy being alone into the wee hours reading or watching TV. But the truth is that I love getting up early in the morning. For me, nothing beats the feeling of being up before everyone else and starting my day fresh, with my mind clear. I have a very busy mind and am prone to anxiety, so my day often gets muddled by my monkey mind the longer it goes on. Because of this, I greatly appreciate the morning hours when things are still fresh and new and clear for me. That is my precious "me time."

For you, however, the best time may be just before you fall asleep. Some people like to have that same kind of quiet, personal moment just before bed, spending some time on the things that matter to their mental, physical, and/or spiritual health. For others, the best time may be mid-afternoon when they can take a break in their busy day. For those with families, that small window of opportunity may happen just before the kids get home. Whatever time of day is best for you, just stick with it. I think you will find that, eventually, it will be something you look forward to and do habitually.

And finally, remember that there is no right or wrong way to honor your gods and goddesses. I cannot sit here and tell you what to do or how to do it. A daily practice is, and should be, highly personal. I can, however, give you at least a small sampling of ideas that you can use to build your own practice. From there, it is up to you and Anubis. Find something that you can do—and stick with it.

Now that we have established what a daily practice is and why it is important, let's consider some of the elements you can use to build that practice—gratitude, meditation, words, music, learning, and witchcraft. Of course, this is not an all-inclusive list. In fact, the possibilities are endless! Here, we'll focus on a few elements that I have incorporated into my own practice over the years, and that I tend to enjoy. And, of course, we'll look at them all in the context of working with Anubis.

Gratitude

Gratitude should be an important part of everyone's daily life, whether or not they have a daily spiritual practice. Gratitude keeps us humble and reminds us of what we have and what is going well in our lives. This is not to diminish the struggles and challenges we experience, but rather to bring a bit of positivity, optimism, and hope into them. I think we can all use a healthy dose of that, with everything that is going on in the world today. And I think gratitude can serve as a great foundation on which to build a daily devotional practice.

When I was a child, I used to spend my afternoons after school with my great-grandmother, who lived next door. I spent countless hours with her and, although she was much older than I was, she was one of my best friends. She had so much life wisdom and I always felt as if I could not get enough of it. We discussed all aspects of life and spirituality, from the concept of god, to kindness, to gratitude, and everything in between. I had a lot of thoughts and musings as a child, and she was always there to help me think them through and process them. One piece of wisdom she shared—perhaps the most important one and one I will always carry with me—is to be grateful for what I have.

Sometimes life's challenges—illness, financial woes, job stress, family pressures, societal changes—can make it hard to be grateful. Of course, I don't want to minimize these experiences. They are difficult and sometimes painful. But pausing for a moment to remind yourself of the good things in your life can be extremely beneficial and can help you cope with all of these challenges by keeping you grounded.

At first, it may be difficult to think of anything to be grateful for, especially if you have a lot going on in your life. That is okay. It is normal, in fact. Don't worry if you have trouble thinking of something for which you can be grateful at first. Many people struggle with this when everything around them feels like chaos. My great-grandmother always told me that, when you cannot find anything to be grateful for, start small. As silly as it may feel, be grateful for the roof over your head. Be grateful for having food to sustain and nourish your body. Be grateful for the job that provides for you and your family.

What does this all have to do with Anubis and building a daily devotional practice? Building a daily practice requires some kind of foundation, an underlying current of understanding that the gods do not have to spend their time with us. They do not have to listen to us or enter our space when invited. They do not even have to receive or welcome any kind of offering left for them. They do not have to care. But I have been shown time and time again that they *do* care—or at least they have in my experience. Are they around 100 percent of the time? No. But, they care. And that is reason enough in itself to bring gratitude into your practice. Remind yourself of this regularly. Reflect on it. And be grateful for how meaningful it is that your gods are a part of your life.

Meditation

Meditation has been the subject of countless books, articles, videos, and audio presentations. People have discussed it, analyzed its benefits, and even given specific guided meditations to help you along your journey. Here I want to focus on the fact that meditation is not just one specific thing. It is not just sitting on a pillow or on the floor with your legs crossed, your eyes closed, and your mind empty. While some prefer that method and find that it works for them, it simply may not work for you or be your preferred method.

Two of the most popular types of meditation are guided meditation and walking meditation. In a guided meditation, you quiet your mind and allow it to follow a path that is laid out beforehand. I have given you an example of a guided meditation at the end of the previous chapter. This can be written, or recorded, or memorized, or read. Alternatively, you may find that a walking meditation works best for you. You'll find one you can try at the end of this chapter. A walking meditation is a mindful walk during which you pay close attention to what you see, hear, and sense around you. This is usually best done away from people in nature.

My favorite way to meditate is with a walking meditation. This makes the experience more calming to me, because it gets me away from the noise and distractions that plague our modern lives and allows me to focus solely on the calming sounds of the natural world around me. Take a long walk in a peaceful setting. See how many different kinds of trees or flowers you can identify. How many different bird songs do you hear? How many different floral, woody, and musty scents do you smell?

When I do a walking meditation, I often find that my brain is much calmer and less "buzzy" with thoughts and worries. And that's when I can focus on Anubis. Many times, on these mindful walks, I like simply to think *about* him—about a specific role he plays or a myth that tells his story. Sometimes I like to imagine I am describing him to others. I tell them who he is, what his powers and influence are, and why he is important to me. I may retell a myth or relate a story about the time that I have spent with him. While this may sound strange to some, I find that it helps to focus my brain and connect me to his energy.

I also like to talk to Anubis during these mindful walks, perhaps having an open, informal conversation with him, as I described in chapter 11. I tell him what I am thinking or feeling, and what he means to me. I discuss my dreams, my hopes, and my aspirations. I thank him for the role he has played, and continues to play, in my life. Of course, I do not expect him to answer me at that moment, but I know that he is listening—or at least is "tuned in," so to speak, to what I am saying. Sometimes I come across a sign—perhaps an animal reminds me of him; perhaps I notice a car license plate with peculiar words or letters; perhaps I see a billboard with a message that is a little too eerily accurate to ignore.

However you reach out to Anubis during your walking meditation, be sure to thank him and perhaps leave a small offering for him.

Words

I love words—spoken words and especially written words. I always have. Ever since I was old enough to hold a pen, I have been a writer. I used to write mini essays as a kid in which I gave my thoughts on a particular topic. I remember writing one for my great-grandmother about how the concept of god transcends just one religion and how there is no right or wrong way to worship. I loved words so much that I studied linguistics in both undergraduate and graduate school and spent a decade teaching languages. I just love to play with words.

Writing is my preferred method of communication. I was a shy child who didn't talk much. As I got older, I began to rely on writing and journaling to sift through my thoughts. Today, I write as a devotional act. It could be a prayer, a poem, or perhaps just "free writing," letting my thoughts on a particular subject flow onto the paper. I find this is very therapeutic for me. I love just sitting down and writing whatever comes to mind. Sometimes this is thoughts on a particular topic; sometimes it ends up being a word dump that leads to something surprisingly profound. I used to encourage my students to free write for ten to fifteen minutes to get their minds going in preparation for writing an essay. There truly is something powerful about it. Profound and meaningful writing can be impromptu.

In the context of a devotional practice, however, you may find that you prefer writing something specific to Anubis. To start with, what you write may be semi-conversational. You may express some of the thoughts you had during a meditative walk, or offer gratitude for his presence in your life. You may write out your thoughts on what death means to you. Or you may wish to reflect on some of the myths and stories discussed in earlier chapters.

Spoken words can also be a devotional act. Some call it prayer, but not all witches and Pagans like that word, perhaps because of its associations with mainstream religions. For me, it's not important what you choose to call it. It's only important that words can be used to converse with deities as part of a daily devotional practice. I have conversations with Anubis daily. I talk to him openly and honestly. For me, this is not a formal process. I do not sit down and write out word for word what I want to say, although sometimes I do that if I intend to use the words in a formal ritual or spell.

We have seen how the ancient Egyptians believed in the power of words and names. Think about the countless words, epithets, and spells etched on the walls of tombs and temples. They imbued the space with power and intention. Anubis's name was inscribed on tomb walls to ensure his guidance and protection. Learn to recognize his name in hieroglyphics (see chapter 1). You may find that you wish to recall it in your head as you communicate with him during prayers, chants, rituals, and spells. As you advance in your relationship with him, you may even learn to write or draw it.

All of the gods in ancient Egypt had a "secret name" that was unknown to most. To know a god's true name meant to have power over him. One myth tells of how Isis tricked Ra into giving her his secret name, thus granting her his power over the sun. She manipulated him into being bitten by a serpent she had crafted from clay and she told him that, in order to heal him, she needed to know his true name. Only when he had given it to her did she cure his body and soul from the serpent's venom.

If you have any interest in writing, even just for your own personal spiritual development and journey, I encourage you to use the journal prompts at the end of each chapter. Below are some other ideas for using writing as part of a daily devotional practice.

- Write a poem about Anubis.

- Write a story about Anubis.

- Journal daily, reflecting on some of the ideas presented in the previous chapter.

- Write lyrics to a song in praise of Anubis.

- Create a "word web" of ideas surrounding Anubis, who he is, and his areas of influence.

- Create a list of words describing Anubis using each letter of his name.

Music

As I have told you, music is a core part of my life. I have music playing throughout my day, practically every single day. My musical tastes are wide-ranging and what I listen to really depends on what mood I am in. I like to listen to upbeat music while I am driving. I listen to something without lyrics with a steady rhythm while I am working. I enjoy listening to something with profound lyrics while sitting with my emotions or feeling in a particular mood. And I often listen to a pop or rock playlist while cooking dinner.

Music can help you connect to your emotions and set your mood. Listening to a sad song can really connect you to difficult experiences you have had in your own life. Listening to an upbeat, happy song can bring more positive emotions out in you. A dear friend of mine once told me to listen to music for the mood I want, not the mood I'm in. And I feel this also applies to the role that music can play in your devotion to the gods. Certain songs definitely make me feel connected to Anubis, or Hekate, or other deities in my life. There are many tracks available today that feature the sounds and themes of ancient Egypt, both with and without words (see below). Find something that really connects you to what you are feeling—perhaps with a good drumbeat that you can focus on, or maybe something softer with a gentle melody.

Make different playlists for different occasions. Build one for when you want to create something—perhaps when you are writing. For me, something with a nice, steady beat, but not too heavy, works well. Make one for when you want to be in a meditative space. For me, this works best with music that has no lyrics. I find that I can get into a meditative state best when the music I play is mostly instrumental or natural sounds. Otherwise, because I love words and language so much, I find myself wanting to focus on the lyrics rather than on quieting my mind.

I am all for making things personal to you and letting your creative side take flight. Make your own music! Drum, sing, or play an instrument. You absolutely do *not* have to be an excellent musician to make music in devotion to your gods and goddesses. You do not even have to go out and buy something. Find a makeshift drum among items around your house—an empty coffee can or even a bucket. What matters most is that you make music as a devotional act and that it comes from a place of meaning and purpose.

If you enjoy singing, even if you do not proclaim yourself to be "good at it," then do that! I absolutely love to sing. I should clarify that. I love to sing *when I am alone*. I do not wish to scare off the neighbors, but that is beside the point. The point is that I love connecting to the energies of the song and belting out the words. It makes me feel as if I am really putting forth my intentions and passion.

In ancient Egypt, priests and worshippers chanted and sang praises to the gods and goddesses as a part of ceremonies and rituals. These were often very purposeful and meaningful, with deep lyrics that praised the gods and petitioned them for a particular cause.

It's easy to incorporate music into a daily devotional practice. Create a playlist on your favorite music platform and name it "Anubis." There are lots of artists out there today you can explore, like the Desert Oasis Ensemble, the Egyptian Meditation Temple, Peter Gundry, and Derek and Brandon Fiechter. Explore music with an Egyptian theme, like *A Ka*

Dua—A Sacred Chant by James Stone. Reach out to meditative music, nature sounds, Pagan music, and witch music. As you listen, identify songs that remind you of Anubis or that have some of the same themes that he does. Add them to your playlist. Listen to them when you are doing your daily practice.

Or better yet, write lyrics to a song about Anubis. Then take it a step further by coming up with a beat. Use drums. Hum. Whistle. Whatever speaks to you. Use this song during your daily devotional practice. However you integrate music into your practice, the gods will be grateful.

Learning

I feel that taking the time to learn something can be a devotional act in itself. When you are learning, you are *literally* devoting your time to expanding your knowledge and awareness and to deepening your understanding of a particular topic. I have always been a firm believer that we never really stop learning. No matter how much we may think ourselves knowledgeable in an area, there is always room to learn more and to deepen our knowledge. And we are never, ever, too old to learn something new. My grandfather was an avid learner even into his advanced years before his passing. He loved learning about the spiritual practices of the indigenous cultures of the Americas. He loved exploring themes like reincarnation, extraterrestrials, and psychic abilities. I seem to have inherited my innate curiosity from him.

Seek out books or articles on spirituality. Look for myths and stories centered around Anubis. There are a lot of good books devoted to Egyptian mythology. As I write, I am working my way through the *Egyptian Book of the Dead*, which is extremely dense and heavy. But it is a learning tool that is helping me better understand how ancient Egyptians may have lived their lives in preparation for the afterlife. There are also books dedicated to Egyptian magick and the worship of Egyptian gods, and a few of these contain small sections about Anubis. I encourage you to check them out as a way to learn more about him and other Egyptian gods and goddesses with whom he is associated. Ancient Egyptian spiritual practices were so interwoven and so intricate that, even if you read about another god or goddess, you may find something that is entirely relevant to your views on Anubis, perhaps in the way a deity was worshipped or its areas of influence.

Here are just a few books that I recommend. You can find more in the Bibliography.

- *The Anubis Oracle: A Journey into the Shamanic Mysteries of Egypt* by Nicki Scully and Linda Star Wolf (Bear & Company, 2008)

- *Shamanic Mysteries of Egypt: Awakening the Healing Power of the Heart* by Nicki Scully and Linda Star Wolf (Bear & Company, 2007)

- *Egyptian Mythology: A Guide to the Gods, Goddesses, and Traditions of Ancient Egypt* by Geraldine Pinch (Oxford University Press, 2002)

- *Ancient Egyptian Magic for Modern Witches: Rituals, Meditations, and Magical Tools* by Ellen Cannon Reed (Weiser, 2021)

- *Ancient Egyptian Magic* by Eleanor L. Harris (Weiser, 2016)

- *Pathworking with the Egyptian Gods* by Judith Page and Jan A. Malique (Llewellyn, 2010)

- *Invoking the Egyptian Gods* by Judith Page and Ken Biles (Llewellyn, 2011)

Witchcraft

Not every Pagan is a witch, and not every witch is a Pagan. I, however, am both, and I incorporate both traditions into my daily practice. If you choose to incorporate witchcraft into your life, either inclusively or exclusively, a daily practice is a great way to devote your time to yourself and to your craft. Then take it a step further and incorporate Anubis into your daily witchcraft practice. Even if you are not a witch, you can still incorporate magick into your daily devotions in a way that makes sense for you and your spiritual path. Most of these practices go beyond labels and can be found across many spiritual traditions worldwide. The most important thing I hope you take from this book is that there is no right or wrong way to honor Anubis and that your devotions should be personal and meaningful to you.

Being a witch is not just about doing elaborate spells and rituals. It is about living a life in which you see the magick in the world around you. It is about utilizing little moments to bring a bit of spice to your life. For me, as a witch, I love "witching up" my day in small ways. Witches are dedicated to learning and growing. They speak their truth and walk their path even when it's challenging. I think this is true for all spiritual paths. You should always find ways to incorporate your spirituality into your daily life in a way that's meaningful and personal to you.

Here are some ways that you can add a bit of "Anubis flair" to your life:

- Celebrate holidays specific to Anubis or incorporate him into holidays you already celebrate (especially Samhain and Yule).

- Perform protection and blessing spells.

- Keep depictions of Anubis around your home.

- Perform rituals that honor the god.

- Practice daily divination to help you cope with the vicissitudes of life.

- Take nature walks.

- Practice guided or walking meditation.

- Read and learn.

- And above all, be your authentic self!

Throughout the previous chapters, I have given you prayers and practices that you can incorporate into your daily devotions. In the chapters that remain, you will find sample offerings, spells, and rituals that can help you deepen your relationship with Anubis.

Walking Meditation to Quiet Your Mind

The human brain loves having something to do and something to think about. The point of a walking meditation is to refocus your brain on something other than the distractions that surround you. One method I use to do this is called the 5-4-3-2-1 method, which engages all your senses and puts you in intimate contact with a peaceful environment.

It is important when doing a walking meditation to pay attention not only to the sights and sounds and smells you encounter but also to where you are and where you are going so that you remain safe. You may also want to bring a small offering for Anubis to thank him for his presence in your life. This should be something that will degrade over time and not do harm to the environment—perhaps a plant or flower, or some small item of food.

Find a quiet spot in nature where you can be alone and undisturbed by the noise and bustle of daily life. If you don't have access to a forest, a lake, or some other isolated setting, you can go to your local park. Begin by taking a few deep breaths and clear your mind.

Look around you and identify five things that you see. Be specific. Notice the bumblebee on the purple flower along the path that is buzzing from one flower to the next. There is a red ribbon tied around that pole over there to the left. Someone lost a button on the path. The sky overhead is dotted with fluffy white clouds. The shadows are lengthening as the sun drops lower on the horizon.

Next, immerse yourself in the sounds around you and identify four things you can hear. A plane just flew by overhead. Children are laughing as they play among the trees. A bird is chirping nearby. A breeze is rustling the leaves on the trees.

Now, take a deep breath and identify three things you can smell. A flower. The scent of pine trees. The musty odor of fallen leaves. Then reach out and touch two things. The rough bark of a nearby tree. The soft leaves of a bush. And finally, concentrate on one thing you can taste. This may be a little trickier. Perhaps you are chewing gum or just had a very garlicky dinner. Or maybe you are wearing cherry-flavored lip gloss.

Focus your mind on the input of all your senses and truly feel a part of the world around you. Then turn your mind inward and open a connection with Anubis. Commune with him; speak to him. Contemplate what he means in your life; offer him thanks for all he has done for you. When you feel ready, thank him for his presence in your life and leave an offering for him.

If you cannot go to a quiet spot in nature, you can do a similar meditation in a more conventional meditative space. You may find that you prefer to do this while seated comfortably at home in your favorite chair or in your backyard. And that is perfectly fine. Tailor the practice to what works best for you. Just be sure that you give yourself a quiet space to focus where there are minimal distractions or interruptions. Use the same 5-4-3-2-1 method to quiet your mind, but focus on the sounds of your home or yard—the dishwasher running, the fan in the window, the sounds of the TV in another room, music playing, the cat scratching on its post, etc.

Journal Prompts

- For at least one week, think of three things every day for which you are grateful. Write them down and be specific. Take it a step further and describe *why* you are grateful for these things.

- Do you already have a daily devotional practice? If so, what does it include? How much time do you devote to it?

- What would you include in a daily devotional practice to honor Anubis?

CHAPTER 13

Offerings to Anubis

You can't go back and change the beginning, but you can start
where you are and change the ending.

C. S. LEWIS

At some point during your journey working with Anubis, you may
decide that you want to take things a little deeper. Now that you have
learned how to identify signs, built communication channels, and developed a daily practice, it's time to think about making offerings to him.
Offerings are simply a way to thank him for being a presence in your life.
They are tokens of gratitude, if you will, for his willingness to guide you
and protect you. Whether you're a new practitioner or an experienced
one, making offerings can be a great way to establish and continue a
relationship with a deity.

You can make offerings to Anubis in exchange for something in
particular. For example, if you ask for his protection during a trip, a
very specific thing, you can leave him a gift of thanks. If you petition
him for healing or for wisdom, you can show him your gratitude with
an offering. On the surface, this may sound a little like "you scratch
my back and I'll scratch yours"—a kind of subtle bribery. But making

offerings is just a way for you to acknowledge that his time, energy, and effort are important and valuable, and that you want to give him something in exchange for that. Think of it almost as fair compensation. The gods—even those seen as benevolent, caring, and giving—deserve to be appreciated for the time and effort that they spend being a part of your life.

Offerings can take many forms—both tangible and intangible. They can be acts of service to a particular cause, or they can be as simple as food or objects that are offered in ritual. But no matter what form your offerings take, remember that they should be personal. I can make suggestions here, but ultimately what matters is that you do something that is meaningful to you. No one likes empty gestures.

Let's begin with acts of service, because I think there are a lot of interesting and unique opportunities there.

Acts of Service

You may not think of many of these intangible ways to give when you think of making offerings, but they hold a lot of value and power. Anubis is a guardian of souls, *all* souls. So reaching out to and supporting those who can use a little extra love, attention, and care is an excellent way not only to honor him but to serve the community.

Volunteering and/or donating your time is a wonderful way to honor Anubis, for instance at a local animal shelter—particularly a dog rescue center. Anubis holds all living things close to his heart, but canines are especially dear to him. Most local animal shelters will never turn down volunteers. They often are looking for people to walk dogs, interact and socialize with animals, play with them, clean their cages, and help with the distribution of medicine and food.

If you can't find the time to volunteer, consider donating to a shelter. I don't think I've ever seen a shelter that didn't need food, towels, newspapers, cat litter, or cleaning supplies. They are always scraping to find enough supplies, because there are often more animals than they have the capacity to care for with the funding that they have. Even spending a few dollars to buy a bag of dog food or donating a few rolls of paper towels can go a long way for dogs and cats that desperately need care. Be sure to check with the shelter before donating to see what their specific needs are and what they accept. Check their website, if they have one, because sometimes they post their needs there.

You may even find shelters for rescued wolves or other canines. Near where I grew up in Indiana, there is a wolf-care facility dedicated to research and education related to these beautiful animals. They always accept donations. They also welcome volunteers, although you may need special training before you can work with the animals in any capacity. Even if you don't work directly with the animals, you may be able to assist in public education programs or by donating to their cause.

And if working with animals isn't your thing, or if you're allergic to dogs, that's totally fine! Don't feel guilty about that, and certainly don't feel that means you can't honor Anubis properly. There are lots of other places where your efforts will be appreciated. Take healthcare facilities, for example. Hospitals and hospice facilities often accept volunteers to serve in a variety of roles. Many hospitals depend on volunteers to act as information clerks, greeters, or gift-shop attendants. Nursing homes often welcome volunteers to socialize with residents. Remember, one of Anubis's chief roles is as a healer. The well-being of *all* creatures is important to him. He is not just some grim reaper looking for the next soul to harvest. His compassion extends to the souls of the living as well.

Likewise cemeteries are an appropriate place to honor Anubis through service because of his associations with the dead and with places connected with them. Cemeteries usually have caretakers, but the extent of the care they deliver may be limited to periodically cutting the grass. Many rural communities simply don't have the resources or manpower to care for smaller cemeteries and, depending on their size and location, funding for their upkeep may just not be available. But those who rest there are just as important as those in the large, freshly manicured cemeteries.

There are lots of small acts of service you can perform in cemeteries, like cleaning up trash and debris. Be sure to check with the local government or institution in charge of the site to determine whether it's acceptable to do that. Cleaning up a cemetery without permission may raise unwanted suspicions, even if it's done with the best of intentions. So please, if this interests you, check with the proper authorities. Cemeteries may be owned by the city or county government, or by a local church. Either way, the local authorities should have a record of ownership.

Leaving flowers on a stranger's grave is another way to give an offering to the Lord of Death, as well as to honor the memory of a dead person's spirit. And you certainly don't need permission to do that! Visit any local cemetery around any patriotic holiday, and you will find people leaving flags and/or flowers at the graves of strangers who were veterans. You can also do this in honor of Anubis by leaving flowers, or even by stopping for just a moment to say a silent prayer for the deceased, even if it's someone you don't know. The grave that you come across with a random name and date may very well belong to someone who was an incredibly fascinating person.

Creative Endeavors

Do you have a creative passion? Singing, playing instruments, dancing, painting, sculpting, crafting, sewing, knitting, weaving, writing, drawing, digital art—these are all areas of artistic endeavor in which many people have talent of some kind. If you have any kind of creative talent, why not dedicate some of that creativity to Anubis? Draw, paint, or sculpt something in his honor and put it on your altar. I've seen some amazing artwork dedicated to Anubis. Although I am not much of an artist myself, I still enjoy doodling and drawing in dedication to him.

Do you play any kind of musical instrument or sing? Dedicate a song to Anubis. It can be something you wrote yourself, or even a song you hear that reminds you of him.

Writing is one of the ways that I connect with Anubis. I write a lot. I love sitting down and crafting something into words in exactly the way that I want it to be expressed. I do a lot of public writing, frequently about Anubis, but I also do a lot of personal writing that never gets published and is kept between me and him. I know a lot of people who write stories and poems dedicated to their chosen deity.

Even if you don't consider yourself to be a creative person, do it anyway! There is always room to try out a new hobby or activity, and you'll get better over time. I am a firm believer that what matters most in honoring a deity is that the effort is meaningful and comes from the heart. So get creative!

Incense

Perhaps the most commonly used offering is incense. Incense can be included in any kind of work with Anubis—or any spiritual work, for that matter. Incense can really enhance the ambiance of a space and help define your intention. It can also be used to purify a space so that it is "reset," in a sense, ridding it of any unwanted energy. The smoke produced by the incense itself becomes sacred.

Anubis has been depicted kneeling next to jars of incense, and incense was often burned as an offering to him. In the embalming tents of ancient Egypt, spaces sacred to him, incense was burned to add to the sacredness of the ceremony and to uplift the spiritual significance of it. It also purified the space so that the priests and embalmers could work properly, and Anubis is referred to on occasion as the Purifier.

Frankincense and myrrh were commonly burned as incense in ancient Egypt, but a particular blend called *kyphi* was sacred and used for a variety of purposes, from medicinal to spiritual. The word *kyphi* comes from a Romanized version of the Greek word for the Egyptian name for the incense, *kapet* (that's a lot!). There are many different versions of it from various parts of the ancient world. A few "recipes" for kyphi have survived, but they all differ slightly, and some are difficult to translate. Some of the common ingredients used include myrrh, honey, wine, raisins, pine resin, pine boughs, cinnamon, cardamom, frankincense, camel grass, juniper berries, and cyperus grass. The result was a blend of sweet, spicy, and musky scents. Kyphi was carefully prepared in a very particular way to bring out the best of the scents of each ingredient, and the process for making it became a sacred ritual itself.

Today, you can buy modern variants of kyphi online. I find that many of these are a beautiful combination of musk and perfume that reminds me of Anubis. A scent called Egyptian Musk is likely intended to be a simplified, diluted variant of kyphi. Some of my personal favorites to burn in offering to him include anything with a spicy, musky scent, like frankincense, sandalwood, myrrh, and cedarwood, although you may find other blends that work well for you.

Other Ritual Offerings

Other ritual offerings to the gods and goddesses include food and drink, stones and crystals, and herbs and plants. The food and drink most commonly offered were bread and beer. This is still true today among modern Kemetic practitioners. Dark beers and ales, as well as dark breads, are frequently offered to Anubis, as are spices like cinnamon or cumin.

One of the symbols most often associated with Anubis is the ankh—a hieroglyphic symbol that represented life, or the breath of life. The mortal life was seen as being just one piece of the journey of the soul, and the ankh represented not only that mortal life, but the afterlife as well. Because of this association, representations of ankhs or actual ankhs make great offerings to Anubis.

Other items used as ritual offerings to Anubis include:

- Aged cheese

- Antique keys and locks

- Artistic drawings or sculptures

- Black coffee or black tea

- Bread, especially darker breads or sourdough

- Cinnamon

- Cold water

- Dark ale or beer

- Dark chocolate

- Dark liqueurs

- Divinations like tarot or oracle card readings

- Frankincense, myrrh, cedarwood, or sandalwood incense

- Items of blue, purple, black, gold, brown, or gray

- Plants like blackberry/bramble, yarrow, sage, lilies, cedar, yew, cypress, elm, pine, acacia, baobab, redwood, or rosemary

- Red wine

- Sacred symbols like the ankh, the Eye of Horus, stars, depictions of skulls or bones, scales, depictions of mummies, bandage wrappings, images of dogs or jackals, sarcophagi, or white feathers

- Stones like obsidian, smoky quartz, hematite, jet, black tourmaline, tiger eye, or clear quartz

Once you've established some ways in which you can make offerings to Anubis, consider setting up a daily practice of offerings to honor the Lord of the Night.

Disposing of Offerings

Disposing of offerings like food and drink or plants may require some thought. You really shouldn't just toss uneaten food into the trash. That just wastes your money and takes up space in landfills. But there are a couple of viable options. The easiest is simply to consume the food yourself. Some people have told me that they consume food offerings as a part of their rituals, once they are finished. In a way, this brings the offering full circle and makes Anubis, who has consumed the energy of the offering, a part of you. Others just leave their offerings somewhere outside, perhaps by a tree, either for animals to eat or to decompose and return to the soil. If you are going to do this, *please* be sure that you don't leave something for the animals that is toxic or highly processed and full of chemicals that may harm them. And don't give the bears your booze!

Above all, remember that all offerings should be personal. Your relationship with Anubis—or with any deity, for that matter—is extremely personal. It will be different from anyone else's, because it is based on your own values, your preferences, your passions, and your life experiences. Even if it is similar to that of other practitioners, it will remain uniquely yours.

It may take some trial and error to find which offerings resonate the most for you. But no matter how you choose to honor Anubis, your devotions are only valid if they are meaningful to you. Anubis isn't going to care whether or not you spend a lot of money on your offerings. He only cares that you are sincere, earnest, and authentic. The rest is entirely up to you.

Ritual Offering to Anubis

Anubis, I offer this ___ to you (name your offering).
May it be a token of my gratitude
For all that you have guided me in
And all that you will guide me in.
Dua Anpu!

Journal Prompts

- Think of at least two or three offerings that you can give to Anubis. What are they?

- Are there any ideas not listed above that you could use?

- What kinds of offerings do you think you will try?

CHAPTER 14

Creating Sacred Space

Your sacred space is where you can find yourself over and over again.

JOSEPH CAMPBELL

As you continue on your journey with Anubis and develop your relationship with him, you may want to consider creating a sacred space dedicated to him. Setting up a sacred space is just one of many ways that you can deepen your practice.

A sacred space can be either physical or ethereal. Physical sacred spaces are places like altars and shrines that you set up and dedicate to your chosen deity. Ethereal sacred spaces are places that you create in your mind's eye or imagination that you can visit when doing any sort of meditational, astral, or journey work.

Sacred spaces, whether physical or ethereal, give you a focused place where you can honor Anubis and focus your intentions on your devotions. They create an environment in which you can set aside other thoughts and feelings, and let yourself connect with the energies, feelings, and thoughts needed at any given time.

Creating a Physical Altar

Perhaps the most common sacred spaces are altars. These are physical places where you can go to pray, do meditations, cast spells, speak to your chosen god, or even leave offerings. In fact, building an altar is a great way to establish a physical space within your home where you can commune with deities and honor them. This will be a place that you can return to whenever you wish to honor your deity—a place where you can leave offerings, do spell work, meditate, or even say a simple daily prayer.

I want to emphasize here that altars don't have to be elaborate and filled with expensive items. They can be as simple or as elaborate as you want them to be. In the day of social media, it's easy to get caught in the trap of comparing yourself to trendy Pagans and witches who appear to have elaborate spaces that feature expensive items and perfect lighting. These spaces may all seem to have the "perfect vibe," but the important thing to remember is that your sacred space must represent your intended purpose.

Altar to Anubis containing statues, stones, and crystals.

Items commonly found on altars include statues of your deity, candles, symbols, stones, and plants. But these are certainly not the only things you can place there. Just remember to keep your altar purposeful and meaningful to you and your deity. Let your intuition lead you to the elements you want to incorporate (see figure on page 138).

If you are dedicating an altar to Anubis, there are many items you can place on it to give it meaning and power, including a statue of the god or an animal related to him, perhaps a wolf or coyote. You can find a wide variety of these statues online and in metaphysical stores. They come in sizes ranging from small to large and in various shapes, colors, and postures. Many of these are quite inexpensive. Feeling creative? Make one out of clay! Or draw a depiction of him that resonates with you. Remember, you don't have to spend any money to honor a deity. What matters above all is that the relationship between you is personal and meaningful.

You can also use a simple photo or piece of artwork in place of (or in conjunction with) a statue—perhaps an image that you drew or painted yourself to give it extra meaning and make it personal. What better way to honor your deity than by creating something in his honor. Draw! Paint! Sculpt! Even a picture of a jackal or wolf will work, especially if you're trying to be a bit more covert in your practice and devotion. Symbols like ankhs are also appropriate.

Or you can dedicate a candle to Anubis, ideally a black and/or gold candle to represent him in his role as the light within the darkness. White candles are also appropriate for most devotional purposes.

If you find that a particular stone has caught your attention, add that. Dark stones and crystals are commonly associated with Anubis, especially if they carry the properties of protection and transformation. Obsidian, smoky quartz, black onyx, labradorite, jet, and hematite are all stones commonly linked to him. You can also include incense, herbs, food and drink, trinkets, or other signs and symbols. If you plan to make offerings on your altar, be sure to include a specific dish or container in which you can place them during rituals. Just remember to keep it simple. Having something that is meaningful to you and dedicated to your deity or spirit is the key. It doesn't have to be elaborate or cost a lot of money.

I am a firm believer in going with your intuition. Of course, there is a time and place for traditional correspondences, but I think that, when it comes to honoring a deity, what *feels* right to you and makes you feel connected to that deity is what's most important.

Not everyone is open with their path, especially when surrounded by family members who may not understand. There is absolutely nothing wrong with that. And the decision of where to locate your altar is a personal choice that sometimes depends on life circumstances. If setting up an elaborate altar in a public space is a problem for you, there are alternative ways to establish some kind of physical sacred space where you can honor the gods in a less conspicuous way. Find a table, shelf, or small corner where you can set aside some space in which you can honor Anubis and connect with him.

I have a decent-sized one-bedroom apartment, so I have "sections" of my home dedicated to particular purposes. In one corner of my main room, I have a desk and a computer dedicated to both my job (I work from home most days) and my writing. In another corner are bookshelves that hold all of my books and a variety of witch tools. Next to these is my altar space dedicated to Anubis. On this, I have included a couple of statues of him along with a dedicated candle, a few stones (labradorite, black onyx, and smoky quartz), and an incense burner. This particular table has multiple shelves. On the lower shelf, I keep the incense I use most often with Anubis, along with the tarot deck I use with him most frequently. I also have a set of Anubis prayer beads that a dear friend gifted to me for Yule several years ago and a couple of pieces of artwork on the wall that depict him in various ways.

Creating an Ethereal Space

Creating an ethereal sacred space can be a little trickier, as it requires a bit of visualization, or at the very least, a bit of imagination and thought. The idea behind an ethereal altar is to create a space that you can visit when doing any kind of meditation, visualization, journeying, trance work, or astral work. Of course, the same principle applies as the one I emphasized above when discussing physical altars—make it personal and meaningful.

I think the best way for me to help you understand ethereal spaces is to show you one. So let's go on a little journey to discover what this kind of space looks and feels like.

Sit somewhere comfortable where you won't be disturbed (or lie down, if that's what you prefer). Speak to Anubis, asking for his guidance as you discover your shared sacred space. I recommend speaking from the heart, but you can adapt the short prayer at the end of this chapter if you prefer.

Close your eyes and take a deep breath, feeling the space in the center of your chest where your lungs expand. Hold it for a few seconds, then release. Continue to breathe slowly, feeling that space fill with air and then releasing it. Let yourself deepen into a relaxed state.

When you feel ready, explore your surroundings with your mind's eye. What do you see? What does this space look like? How big is it? What is it made of? How is the lighting? What objects do you see? What colors surround you? Are there any figures or guides there with you? Do you hear anything? Smell anything?

I cannot answer any of these questions for you. Rely on your mind's eye to discover what is there. You may find that there isn't much there yet, but that's okay. You get to decide what belongs there and where it goes. In the same way that you created a physical space, you get to "decorate" your ethereal space in any way you choose! This space is meant to be a meaningful place to which you can return whenever you want to visit and commune with Anubis.

Of course, not everyone can visualize or meditate in this way. And remember, there are different ways to meditate that are appropriate for different purposes. Many people have trouble with the kind of visualization described above, and that's perfectly fine. You don't have to be skilled at visualization to honor Anubis or even to create a sacred space in honor of him.

One alternative is to draw or paint your ethereal space. Don't worry if you're not an artist. This is meant for you and Anubis. Just sit down with a blank piece of paper and colored pencils, crayons, markers, chalk, or paint—whatever you prefer. Take a moment to relax and take a few deep breaths. Then ask for Anubis's guidance in creating your sacred space. Then let your imagination take control!

Don't think too much about it. Create what comes to mind without hesitation. Even if something comes to mind that you may not immediately feel is connected to Anubis, go with it. That's the beauty of having a personal experience with a deity. Each one is unique. What you see in your mind's eye may or may not be the same as what others see. Don't feel that what you envision has to meet certain expectations or have a certain look or feel to it. Remember—it's personal.

Maintaining Your Sacred Space

It's important to maintain your sacred space—whether it's physical or ethereal—by keeping it clean and renewing its power.

Cleaning your physical altar space can be an act of devotion in itself. Take time to remove items from it. Clean the surface. Dust off any statues or objects that you keep there. Soft-bristled toothbrushes can work wonders to clean tiny cracks, ridges, and crevices in statues, amulets, and stones. You can also use non-corrosive oils to polish and anoint them. Then, intentionally return each item to the altar, reaffirming its place and meaning.

For your ethereal altar, the more you revisit it, the more it becomes ingrained in your mind and the stronger it becomes. Mentally revisit this sacred space often. Go through the same steps you went through to create it. Ask yourself the same questions about what you see, hear, feel, and smell. You may discover new details that you didn't notice before. The more you revisit it, the clearer and more defined it may become. And the more power it will have. That's part of the beauty of it.

In the end, there's no right or wrong way to create or maintain your sacred space. Whether you choose to create a physical altar, an ethereal space, or both, make sure that what you create is something personal and intentional. It doesn't have to look a certain way. Remember, not everyone can visualize these spaces easily, and there is absolutely nothing wrong with that. Work with your strengths. Rely on your creativity, your imagination, and your intention. And above all, make it meaningful to you.

Prayer to Create Ethereal Sacred Space

Anpu,
Great Guide to the Spirit Realm,
May your eyes pierce the darkness
To show me the way,
To lead me to a sacred space
Where I may honor you
And connect to your energies and wisdom.
Protect me on this journey and in this space,
O Guardian.
Dua Anpu!

Journal Prompts

- Do you already have an altar dedicated to your spiritual practice? If so, what's on it?

- Describe what your sacred space might look like in honor of Anubis.

- Brainstorm some ideas that you can include in your sacred space, either physical or ethereal.

CHAPTER 15

Making Magick

I thought: "I cannot bear this world a moment longer."
"Then child, make another."

MADELINE MILLER, CIRCE

Magick was an integral part of ancient Egyptian society. In modern spiritual practice, magick is practiced by those who, like me, identify as witches. But even if you do not identify as a witch, the energy of magick still exists in everything around you, and many other spiritual paths incorporate it in some way. It is woven into the fabric of reality—into every plant, animal, person, tree, and rock. It swirls in the sea, dances in the flame, and soars through the air. We feel it in the rays of the sun and seek it in the glow of a moonlit starry night. Although intangible and invisible, it is palpable and even malleable. It is this energy that witches, shamans, druids, and spell casters weave into their lives and use to heal, to support, to change, to grow, to adapt, and even to destroy.

It is in this weaving that we find spellcraft. Casting spells is a way to bring about transformation and influence outcomes. It's a way for practitioners to work with the spirits of the natural world to instigate change. Spells can create, heal, attract, change, or destroy. You may hear about "good" and "bad" spells, but the truth is that spells themselves are neither good nor bad. Spellcraft is always neutral. It's simply a tool. It's the practitioners who use spells for good or evil who make the ultimate decision about how to direct their energy. They can choose to create and to heal, or to curse and destroy.

In this chapter we'll explore how magickal practices like spells, amulets, charm bags, scrying, and divination can be used to call on the powers of Anubis.

Casting Spells

Making magick does not have to be expensive. I am all for using what you have on hand rather than going out and buying something. You don't need to have fancy, shiny tools to perform effective witchcraft. It's your intention that matters most. Witches with a strong intention to do something are a powerful force. So there is no need to go out and buy an expensive candle holder and fifteen different-colored candles, one for every possible occasion. Nor do you need to buy out an entire apothecary's stock of oils and herbs.

That being said, witchcraft *is* a craft, and there is just as much power in the planning of a spell as there is in performing the actual spell itself. Deciding what tools and ingredients you are going to use really sets the stage for any working. When you clarify your ideas and set your intentions, you can be more effective at weaving them into your spell. But that does not mean that, if you don't have a black candle on hand and have to use a white one, your spell will fail or that you are doing it incorrectly. Yes, it's important that you be intentional. But be intentional with what is available to you and what feels best.

Below, you'll find spells that you can use to invoke Anubis or to draw on his powers as a guide and protector. I have intentionally *not* included any baneful spells, curses, hexes, or negative workings. This doesn't mean that I disapprove of them, or that I never do them. It's just that I don't feel they are appropriate for this book, nor do they demonstrate how I personally work with Anubis. There are plenty of other sources where you can find them, if you want them.

Here are a few tips for casting spells:

- White candles work for every occasion.

- Substitutions can come in handy. There are many stones that function similarly, and the same can be said for herbs and plants.

- Repurpose items you have around the house—like that candle holder that has been sitting in the back of your cupboard for years.

- Save those jars! They come in handy for storing ingredients and as spell jars.

- Gather your own plants and herbs if you can, rather than buying them. On the other hand, it's okay to buy them if you prefer.

- All herbs and plants in the spells below are meant to be fully dried before use.

- Do not forget to thank any spirits or deities that you invite to your spell work and always leave an offering to them.

- If your spells don't work, that doesn't mean that you are a failure. There are a multitude of reasons why a spell might fail. Sometimes *not* getting what you think you want is exactly what you actually need. And sometimes it may simply be that what you want is not meant to happen at that point in time.

Protection Spells

Anubis is an incredibly protective god. His charge in ancient Egyptian myths was to guide and protect the souls of the dead, and the living petitioned him for guidance and protection in their lifetimes so that, in the afterlife, they might find peace. You can invoke his protection for yourself, your family, your home, or your pets. Here are some examples.

Spell to Protect Yourself

This is a very short and simple spell that you can perform when you do not have a lot of time. I use this on a pretty regular basis, especially before I do any traveling or when I feel that I might need a bit of extra protection.

To perform this spell, you will need:

- Bay leaf

- Black candle

- Black marker

- Fire-safe container

- Oil like frankincense or sandalwood

Using your fingers, anoint the candle with the oil, then light it. As you do so, ask for Anubis to be present during your spell work. On the bay leaf, either draw a protective symbol like an ankh or another symbol that is meaningful to you, or write a short affirmation, like, "I am protected." Hold the bay leaf in your hand and ask Anubis to protect you. Say or chant the following seven times:

Anubis of Obsidian,
Anubis of Black,
Anubis of Night,
Protect my body, mind, and spirit,

With the flame of the candle, light the bay leaf and place it in the fire-safe container. Picture yourself wrapped in a bubble of protective energy that flows from Anubis's hands. Imagine this strong energy encasing you in his impenetrable power. Let it surround you and hold you there for a moment.

When you are finished, give thanks to Anubis and dispose of the ashes in an eco-friendly manner.

Spell Jar to Protect the Home

Spell jars are incredibly powerful ways to create a concentrated intention for protection. When you create a spell jar, you place in it items that correspond to your intention—including plants, stones, or minerals, but also sometimes symbolic objects. You can create these jars for a variety of purposes, and place them around your house or bury them, depending on your intention. Leave them in place, either until they've served their purpose, or until they need to be refreshed or redone.

To create this spell jar, you will need:

- Basil leaves

- Black peppercorns

- Black candle

- Incense, preferably sandalwood or frankincense

- Pinch of mugwort

- Salt

- Pine, juniper, or cypress boughs

- Clear quartz crystal

- Sprig of rosemary

- Sprig of sage leaves

- Small clean jar

Close your eyes and take a few deep breaths to get yourself into a centered, calm space. Light the candle and then the incense. Invite Anubis to work with you using this prayer:

Anubis, Lord of Protection,
Guardian of All,
I invite you here in this space.
Dua Anpu!

Hold the jar upside down over the incense and let the smoke fill it. If you are using stick incense, place it in the jar. Swirl the smoke around nine times and let it permeate the jar. As you do, say:

Anubis, guard and protect me.

Place the jar back on your altar—or whatever you are using as a work surface—along with the incense, letting it continue to burn while you do your work. Then place a layer of salt in the bottom of the jar while saying:

Anubis, guard and protect me.

Add the clear quartz crystal and the peppercorns while saying:

Anubis, guard and protect me.

Next, add the plants and herbs one by one, between each one saying:

Anubis, guard and protect me.

As you add them, imagine the energy of each adding to the overall protective energy of the jar. When you are finished, put the ashes from the burned incense into the jar, letting them fall as they may around the other contents. Say:

Anubis, guard and protect me.

Place the lid on the jar and tighten it.

Hold the black candle so that the wax drips around the edges of the lid of the jar, letting it harden to create a seal. You may want to put down a cloth or towel before doing this to avoid any wax hardening on your work surface. Repeat the phrase "Anubis, guard and protect me" until you have a seal of thick wax around the jar lid.

When the wax is hard, hold the jar in both hands in front of you and close your eyes. Feel the energy of the jar pulsating in your hands. Add your own energy to it. Imagine a flow of energy passing down your arms, through your hands, down your fingertips, and into the jar. Every item in the spell jar has been carefully added to create protection. Feel that. While still holding the jar in both hands, ask for Anubis's blessing, saying:

Anubis, Obsidian Lord,
Great Protector of All,
Cloak of black, eyes of gold,
As I cast this spell,
I ask that you imbue this jar
With your protective energy.
May its contents protect me and this home.
May its energies protect and guard me and my home
And all that rests within.
May no unwanted, ill-intended, or negative energies enter.
May it be so.

Dua Anpu!

Place the jar in a safe place in your home—ideally by the entryway or in your bedroom. Or you can bury it outside your door for a bit of hidden magick.

When you are done, thank Anubis for aiding you in your work and leave him an offering. You may find that you need to refresh or re-make the jar as time goes by.

Spell to Ward Off Evil

Many cultures believe that doors and windows are not only physical entry points, but also portals through which spiritual energies and spirits may enter. One way to protect your home is to create a protective barrier around it using protective symbols on the doors and windows.

Start by choosing a symbol that resonates with you. I like to use the ankh, for example, because I do a lot of protection spells with Anubis. The ankh has a lot of different meanings, and one of them is protection. You can also use the Eye of Horus or a pentagram.

Dip the index finger of your dominant hand into an oil like sandalwood, frankincense, or cedarwood to give your spell a little extra "oomph." Draw your chosen symbol on the doors of your home. Imagine that it glows brightly in shades of dark blue, dark purple, and black.

You may not want to put oil directly on your windows because it may leave a streak. But you can either draw your symbol on the window frame or (and this is my recommendation) do the spell without the oil. Simply draw the symbol and imagine it glowing brightly as you did before.

Imagine that a barrier of energy extends from each symbol, spreading over every wall, into every corner, and across the ceiling and floors, until they are connected and form a protective barrier. Then petition Anubis for his protection, saying:

Great Lord Anpu,
Grant this home your obsidian shroud.
Cloak this home in your protection.
May none enter who wish harm.
May unwanted energies be banished.

May we be safe.

Hail Anpu!

For an extra bit of power, place dark stones like obsidian, jet, or black tourmaline in the corners of your home.

Always be sure to leave an offering to Anubis for his protection. And re-do this spell at least monthly—more frequently if needed—to ensure that your home is always protected.

Spell to Protect a Deceased Pet

At your pet's gravesite, or in your home near a photo of your pet, light a white or gold candle to represent the light within the darkness, the light within the grief and pain that you are experiencing. You may wish to bring a favorite toy or perhaps your pet's collar and place it near the candle.

As you do, ask for Anubis's protection of your beloved pet:

Hail Anubis Psychopompos!
Usher of Souls,
Guardian of the Departed,
____ (your pet's name) has crossed over into your realm.
Although grieving I am,
I know he/she is in your care.
Look after him/her, protect him/her, guide him/her.
May he/she reach the fields of everlasting happiness and peace
And may he/she feel loved and secure.

Amulets and Blessing Spells

Amulets are great ways to protect yourself from unwanted energies, to call down blessings, and to connect to a particular deity or spirit. Ancient Egyptians wore them to protect themselves in this life and in the afterlife. Many depicted Anubis. Wear a symbol that you associate with Anubis—like the ankh, the Eye of Horus, or a key—to remind you that you carry his protective energy wherever you may go.

Blessing to Set a Daily Intention

This spell is just one of those small ways you can "witch up" your life and set your intention for the day. Setting your intention for the day when you first get up in the morning can be a powerful way to align your thoughts and energies with what you want to accomplish that day. Of course, there are myriad things that can derail you altogether. But starting your day with intention can make a world of a difference in how it turns out. If you aren't sure what you want to accomplish for the day, set your intention to have a happy, healthy one.

First, fix your favorite morning beverage. For me, it's black coffee with a dash of non-sugar sweetener. Hold the mug in one hand and place your other hand above it. Draw an ankh above the mug, imagining it descending into the mug and imbuing your beverage with the energy of your desires. State your intention for the day, asking Anubis to assist you:

Anubis, be with me.

This mug I bless

That my day may be filled with my desire.

As you drink your beverage, imagine your body and spirit being filled with your intention.

Ritual Bath

Ritual baths can be done for a variety of purposes, but in general, they are done to reconnect to your spiritual self. They often involve cleansing the body both physically and energetically, and blessing it so that you may be the best version of yourself that you can be. They also provide a good opportunity for self-care.

Prepare a bath for yourself. If you like, add essential oils. Just make sure that they are safe to use and aren't going to cause a skin reaction. If it's safe to do so, light a white candle near your tub. You can also add stones. Give yourself time to relax in this bath. Do some deep breathing exercises. Ask Anubis to be present with you.

Wash your body as you normally would, imagining that you are not only cleansing your physical body but also washing away any unwanted energy. Then anoint various parts of your body by touching them with a dab of oil, as described below. Sandalwood, frankincense, or even rose or lavender to reflect calm and loving energy work well. Use what feels best to you at the time.

As you anoint your feet with oil, say:

Anubis, bless my feet that I may walk a path
of integrity and authenticity.

Anoit your hands, saying:

Anubis, bless these hands that weave magick and do the work daily.

Touch your chest at your heart center, saying:

Anubis, bless my heart that I may show compassion
toward myself and others.

Touch your throat, where your throat chakra is located, saying:

Anubis, bless my voice so that I may always speak my truth.

Touch your forehead at your Third Eye, saying:

Anubis, bless me with the sight to see what is unseen.

Finally, touch the top of your head, your crown chakra, saying:

Anubis, bless me so that I may know what is unknown.

When you are finished, thank Anubis for being present.

Blessing to Protect a Pet

Of course, Anubis has a soft spot for dogs, but all animals are sacred to him and you can call on him to bless any kind of pet.

Place a photo of your pet next to a white candle. If your pet is nearby, you can caress it softly. Just be sure it stays safely away from the candle. If at any point your pet becomes uncomfortable, don't force it to stay.

As you light the candle, imagine a bubble surrounding your pet made of various colors—red, blue, orange, green, purple, and even white.

While you do this, call out to Anubis to ask him to guide your pet:

Anubis, Lord of the Dog Star,
Celestial Jackal,
He who is between Light and Shadow,

> *Protect _____ (your pet's name).*
> *Guide him/her and guard him/her.*
> *May he/she be ever safe in your presence.*

Divination

Anubis was petitioned for spiritual guidance and divinatory purposes, especially during the times of Greek and Roman influence. He can be a powerful spiritual guide, and he can be petitioned for granting visions. Any kind of divinatory work in which you consult the divine or the spirit world can be done with his aid, including using charm bags, receiving dream messages, and scrying. Here are a few practices for you to try.

Charm Bag for Spiritual Guidance

Charm bags can be simple but powerful tools for bringing a bit of magick into your everyday life in a way that is transportable. They are usually filled with a combination of herbs, stones, and/or charms with related correspondences that you put together for a specific purpose. You can create a charm bag for protection, for abundance, for love, for intuition, or for any number of other purposes. This is an example of one to bring spiritual guidance from Anubis.

To make this charm bag, you will need:

- Amethyst
- Laurel leaves
- Obsidian
- Small charm of Anubis or a small ankh
- Cloth bag—you can get these online or at most metaphysical stores
- Yarrow

Place the items into the bag one by one, imagining them imbuing the bag with their energies. Hold the bag in both hands and ask for Anubis's blessing:

Anubis, Keeper of Keys,
Unlock the secrets for me
To a deeper, meaningful life.
Guide me to the doors I need to open.
Lead me along my path.

Carry this bag in your pocket or keep it somewhere where you'll see it often. Periodically remind yourself of your intention and call to Anubis for guidance.

Petition for Dream Messages

Anubis was often petitioned for guidance through messages received in dreams. You can do this yourself by placing a piece of amethyst or smoky quartz under your pillow or near your bed at night before you retire. You can also add a piece of rose quartz for a little calming energy, as some (like me) are very sensitive to amethyst. Be sure to set yourself up for sleeping well. Go to bed at a decent hour. Spend the last hour of your evening without any screens. Have a cup of chamomile tea. Do a quick relaxing meditation.

Before you fall asleep, ask Anubis to grant you a dream that contains a message about something you need to know. Pay attention in the dream to what symbols stand out to you and what you see, hear, and feel. Is anyone present in the dream? If so, what do they say to you? Keep your journal nearby to record what you remember when you wake up.

Scrying for Guidance

Scrying is a divination method that has been used for thousands of years in cultures around the globe. It involves gazing into either a bowl or body of water or a mirror, and allowing visions and messages to come to you. It's similar to the idea of gazing into a crystal ball or watching the flames of a fire dance. In ancient Greece and Rome, Anubis was often petitioned through scrying.

Use a medium-sized bowl made either of clear glass or some reflective metal like copper, silver, or bronze. Fill the bowl with water and place it on a table that is at a comfortable height for you to peer into it. You can do this either sitting or standing, whatever is most comfortable for you. Put a few drops of oil into the bowl—something like rose, lavender, or sandalwood.

Place your hands over the bowl, close your eyes, and ask Anubis to grant you a vision:

Anubis, Master of Secrets,
Let me peer into the Mysteries.
Grant me a vision.
May I see into the unseen
And know the unknown.

Repeat this three times, then open your eyes and take a few deep, centering breaths. Gaze into the bowl and let yourself sink into a relaxed state. Let your vision soften and become unfocused as you do. You may find that images, ideas, and thoughts come to mind. Don't force them; let them come to you as they will. Be mindful of anything you see, hear, think, or feel. Record anything that comes up in your journal when you are finished.

Journal Prompts

- Start a record of the spells you cast. Keep this *Book of Shadows* near your altar as a record of your work.

- If you use magick in your spiritual work, how can you refocus it to support your work with Anubis?

CHAPTER 16

Celebrations

Remember that life is a series of what you may call challenges,
but these are not in continuous motion. There have to be periods of
quiet reflection. Time to think, breathe, and feel, and to understand
how far you have travelled on this, your journey.

JUDITH PAGE AND JAN A. MALIQUE, *PATHWORKING WITH THE EGYPTIAN GODS*

Figuring out which days were "holy days" or "feast days" in ancient Egypt is incredibly complicated because we don't really have any good sources on which to rely. One challenge is that it's difficult to pinpoint exactly how the Egyptian calendar corresponded to the Gregorian calendar, so it's hard to know exactly when feast days and holy days were celebrated. To add to the confusion, Egypt had multiple calendars and they changed multiple times.

A lunar calendar that is thought to be one of the older Egyptian calendars contained months that were twenty-nine to thirty days long and began at the New Moon. Later, a calendar was developed that followed the flooding cycles of the Nile. These cycles were essential to the ordering of their society because they determined when crops were planted and harvested each year.

There were three seasons in the Egyptian year that lasted for four months each, for a total of around 360 days. But there were also five extra days that were dedicated to the five most important gods and goddesses—Osiris, Isis, Nephthys, Seth, and Horus. The year began around the time that Sirius, the Dog Star, became visible above the horizon of the night sky and the flooding of the Nile began (see chapter 9).

Later in Egyptian history, a civil calendar came into use based on a year broken into months, weeks, days, and hours. But this calendar was a fraction of a day different from their solar calendar. As a result, over time, the beginning of the new year no longer corresponded with the flooding of the Nile. Because of all this confusion, modern historians have difficulty coming up with exact dates and times for events in Egypt that correspond precisely with our calendar.

But this doesn't mean that we can't celebrate important days in Egyptian lore. Remember, this experience is supposed to be personal. So you should celebrate and honor Anubis when it makes sense to you, even if that date doesn't "align" with the date on which ancient Egyptians celebrated him. When we incorporate deities into our work as modern practitioners, we should do so in a way that makes sense to us and our lives. Some speculate that Anubis's feast day fell between May 6 and May10, but if you want to make him a part of your Samhain celebration—great! Do that. Do you want to honor him during a particular month? Awesome. Celebrations are highly personal and should be treated as such. Honor Anubis when it makes the most sense to you and your practice. Besides, themes surrounding death and the mysteries of the world are relevant no matter what time of the year it is.

In Appendix B, you'll find a list of a few days that I associate with Anubis, along with my own experiences and thoughts about them. This is not, by any means, a complete list, but it will give you a good sense of some of the days on which you can incorporate celebrations to honor Anubis into your spiritual practice.

Solstices and Equinoxes

The solstices and equinoxes—sometimes called "quarter days"—are days that mark the turning of the Wheel of the Year. The summer and winter solstices mark the days on which the sun is at its most southerly and most northerly points in the sky relative to the equator, resulting in the longest and shortest days of the year, respectively. The spring and fall equinoxes mark the days on which the sun is directly above the equator, resulting in days and nights of roughly equal length.

In chapter 9, we learned that Anubis was particularly celebrated around the summer solstice, when he was said to visit the necropoli. Unfortunately, little is known about this celebration, but we can speculate that it was probably associated with honoring the dead and remembering loved ones who had passed on, because it was thought that the veil between our world and the spirit world was at its thinnest on these quarter days.

Personally, I associate Anubis with all four seasonal markers. I associate him with the light within the darkness at winter solstice, and the shadows within the light at the summer solstice. During the spring and fall equinoxes, there is a balance between light and darkness, making it the perfect time to celebrate the Liminal Lord himself. I honor Anubis particularly at the equinoxes because of his roles associated with balance between light and dark, life and death, and the celestial realm and the Underworld.

All four of these quarter days are harbingers of change closely tied to the celestial bodies, particularly the sun and its impact on the world. They mark points of transformation, when the shifting of the balance between light and darkness occurs. Because Anubis, as Lord of Death, is the master of transformation, these holidays are a perfect time to celebrate him.

I really value these quarter days, because nature and the natural cycles of the world are important to me. That's why I love to spend time in nature on these days. I love looking at the great cycle of waxing and waning light through the lens of change and transformation, and incorporating Anubis in these seasonal celebrations is a powerful way to really dive deeply into this theme. Here are a few ideas for honoring him on the quarter days:

- Do a ritual honoring Anubis as Liminal Lord and Lord of the Death.

- Go for a walk in nature and leave an offering to Anubis.

- Write in your journal about the idea of balance and change.

- Create a sigil representing the balance of light and dark.

- Light candles of contrasting colors—black and white, or black and gold.

- Cast spells that deal with change and transformation.

At the end of this chapter, you'll find a spell for honoring Anubis at the equinox.

Seasonal Celebrations

In addition to the solstices and the quinoxes, there are other days through-out the year that were traditionally marked by rituals and celebrations. For instance, the rising of Sirius, known as the Dog Star, was honored in rituals associated with Anubis (see chapter 9). The term "dog days of summer" refers to the hottest, harshest days of the year when the sun is at its peak. In the Northern Hemisphere, these typically start anywhere between July 3 and mid-August and last anywhere from thirty to sixty days. In the times of ancient Rome, the lethargy caused by the scorching heat was blamed on Sirius.

Anubis was also honored during what was known as "Scorpio season," which lasted roughly from October 22 to November 21, depending on the year and the movement of the planets and stars. Scorpio represents transformation and change, so Scorpio season aligns perfectly with Anubis in his role as Lord of Transformation.

If you are a Scorpio (like me), you understand the cycles of transformation. Life has many of these cycles and Scorpios not only understand them, but can really embrace them and make them their own.

Here are some ways you can honor Anubis during Scorpio season:

- Leave daily offerings.

- Make a commitment to doing daily shadow work.

- Cast spells involving transformation.

- Write in your journal about shadow work or transformation.

Celebrations of Life

When a loved one passes on, it's common to hold some kind of remembrance. One practice that's becoming increasingly popular is called a "celebration of life." This is a time to celebrate the positive aspects of people's lives by honoring their memory and who they were as individuals. These often include the sharing of photos, stories, music, and mementos associated with the deceased. They focus on keeping their memory alive and celebrating who they were rather than on the grief of those left behind. During these celebrations, you can petition Anubis to be present and ask for protection for the deceased. If you want to be a bit more covert, you can simply light a single candle that you've dedicated to Anubis beforehand and ask for his presence.

Ritual to Honor Anubis at the Equinox

This ritual can be performed at either the spring or autumn equinox. If you plan to perform it during in the spring, do it at dawn to symbolize that the light will be growing from that point forward. If you are performing it in the autumn, do it at dusk to symbolize the darker half of the year that is approaching.

To perform this ritual, you will need:

- Two candles of contrasting colors, either black and white, or black and gold

- Incense

- Frankincense or sandalwood oil

Place the two candles symbolizing the darkness and the light on your altar. Anoint them with frankincense or sandalwood oil and ask Anubis to bless them.

Light the candles, starting with the candle representing darkness, and say:

Anubis, Liminal Lord,
Lord of Darkness and Light,
One who rests in the in-between spaces,
I praise you.

During this in-between time,
May I not forget the lesson of balance.
Light dances with darkness to wax and wane,
Each different, but in perfect unison,
Each ever-present, each ever-needed.
Guide me and protect me as I go forward.

Meditate as you let the candles burn out.

Journal Prompts

- Do any of these celebrations speak to you?

- Are there any other festivals or holidays that you already celebrate in which you could incorporate Anubis in some way?

CHAPTER 17

Shadow Work

"What is it that you want from me?" I asked Anubis. The room was dark, with just enough light to see him in front of me, but I was neither cold nor afraid. The darkness was almost comforting.

Anubis did not answer, but I knew that I was to follow him. He led me to a door at the end of a dark corridor and said: "Open it. This is the door to your inner self, the deepest parts of your mind. In it, you will find your hopes, dreams, and desires, but also your fears and the parts of you that need healing."

Without another word, I knew that Anubis wanted me to heal. The Great Shaman was there to show me the way down that path.

ANUBIS TO ME DURING A MEDITATION

This was just the beginning of what has been my lifelong journey of working to be a better version of myself, to face my shadow and accept it as a part of who I am. It was the beginning of my journey to heal the wounds I had been carrying from the traumas I'd faced over the years. Anubis has been with me ever since I started down this Pagan path well over two and a half decades ago. And yet, as the years go by, I find that we continue to go deeper.

Anubis is the god of death and rebirth, but not just in a literal sense. He protects us as we go through those cycles in life in which something old that no longer serves us falls away, leaving something new and often better in its wake (although perhaps not at first). He guides us through dark times and helps us come out the other side "reborn." As shaman and healer, he helps us find those pieces of ourselves that are lost or in need of healing. He brings us out of the shadow and into the light. And this is the essence of shadow work.

From Darkness to Light

Shadow work consists of a journey into the dark corners of your mind and your emotions—the places that harbor the feelings and memories you don't necessarily want to face—and bringing them into the light so that they can be healed. This is the difficult work required to free yourself from emotional pains and traumas.

Giving yourself the opportunity to heal can be an extremely painful process. When you reach within yourself to bring up old emotional wounds, the experience can be just as gut-wrenching as it was when you first felt them. But repressing those feelings—even though it may seem easy in the short term—does you no good in the long run. I can tell you from personal experience that past traumas and emotional wounds will return to rear their ugly heads sooner or later. And sometimes they can be even more powerful than they were when they originally occurred. When you fail to confront these shadow aspects of yourself, it can affect your own happiness and well-being, and negatively impact your relationships with those around you as well. It can hold you back and keep you feeling as if there is a perpetual weight on your shoulders.

Working with Anubis to confront your shadow can be incredibly powerful. He can guide you on shamanic journeys that take you into the dark recesses of your mind and lead you back to the light. He can teach you how to heal yourself by shining light on the darker areas of your life. You can meet him during meditations and journeying. You can ask for guidance through divination. You can do spell work with him, or you can simply pray to him for guidance and protection.

It is really up to you how you choose to integrate Anubis into your shadow work. But it's very important to note that he isn't just going to take your pain away. It doesn't work like that. You have to put in the work. This work isn't easy, but having Anubis by your side can help you to feel safe and protected on your journey and make it more meaningful for you.

A note of caution: I am not trained or licensed as a therapist, a psychiatrist, or a mental-health professional, nor do I profess to be. I have no experience providing therapeutic or pharmaceutical treatment of any kind. But I am someone who has had to process a lot of grief and trauma in my life, and that has made me a strong advocate of shadow work. All that I share with you here comes from my own personal experiences, combined with the reading and research that I've done over the years. But I know from that experience that spiritual shadow work or any of its practices are *not* a substitute for treatment by a trained professional, and I strongly advise everyone to seek therapy and/or medication when appropriate. Shadow work can be one tool to address mental-health issues, but it should never be seen as a replacement for conventional treatments. Sometimes seeking the help of a professional *is* the work, and is exactly what you need to support you on your healing journey.

The Three "Bs"

There are three things that are important to remember when doing any kind of shadow work: *Be safe. Be grounded. Be patient.*

The first and most important is to stay safe. If at any point during your healing journey (or any time, really), you have thoughts about harming yourself or others, please seek help immediately. In the United States, you can call 9-8-8, the number for the National Suicide and Crisis Lifeline, or 9-1-1 to reach your local emergency system. Shadow work can often bring up painful, sometimes traumatic, memories. There is no shame in this. We all sometimes need help that we cannot provide for ourselves, and that is okay.

The next is to stay grounded. When doing any kind of exploratory work with old wounds, be sure you're in a safe, comfortable space, either sitting or lying down. Grab your favorite blanket and a soft pillow. Hug a stuffed animal. Whatever makes you feel comfortable and safe, because this will help keep you grounded. Make sure you are somewhere where you won't be bothered by sudden noises or loud sounds, as these can be distracting when attempting any kind of meditative or mind-body-emotion work. Always have water and a snack nearby, ideally something that is high in protein, like almonds. This may sound trivial, but it's important. When you're going through a lot of intense emotions, having something nearby that can help bring you back into your body when you're finished is important.

And finally, remember the old adage: "Rome wasn't built in a day." Be patient. I can't stress enough how important this is. Processing your feelings and healing take time. It's not a "one and done" thing. Unlike physical ailments, mental and emotional pain does not come with a time-stamp. You can usually make a rough estimate of how long it will take to heal a broken leg. There are exceptions, of course, and a multitude of factors can play into that process. But, for the most part, doctors can estimate how long it will take based on their understanding of the human body and the available medical treatments.

But emotional healing is non-linear. Memories of trauma and mental abuse, for example, may come up time and time again, even when you are sure that you have "dealt with them." This is because the impacts of these past experiences are hidden deep in the recesses of your mind where they can have a pervasive effect. Your mind will continue to revisit them because it was trained to think, feel, and react in a certain way. Unlearning that training and moving beyond how your mind was conditioned to react is an incredibly difficult process that can take years, and even then those impacts may linger.

Take time to *feel* your emotions and let them come to the surface. That is the first step toward healing. Don't let your thoughts or judgments get in the way. Don't analyze your feelings. As uncomfortable as it may be, you have to just sit with them for a moment. We spend too much time fighting against our emotions and labeling them as "bad" or "wrong." We tell ourselves that we shouldn't be feeling this way, and that conviction keeps us from moving forward by dismissing our feelings as invalid before we even begin to process them.

It may take some practice to learn how to feel into your emotions, because most of us are accustomed to analyzing them. But that practice is well worth the effort. We all have the tendency to avoid what is uncomfortable, but I can tell you from personal experience that this doesn't help. No matter how many times you push down your emotions, ignore them, and pretend they aren't there, they will eventually resurface (sometimes with a vengeance) and continue to wreak havoc in your life.

Confronting Your Shadow

Allowing yourself to feel your emotions is the best way to start your journey out of the shadow and into the light. When doing shadow work, you may encounter feelings and emotions that you may not connect with any particular circumstance or event in your life. You may just know that you feel a certain way and that it's uncomfortable. And that's okay. But this may leave you with a desire to gain an understanding of where those feelings originated. And that's okay, too. Let yourself explore them, but don't label them. Don't make judgments. Don't analyze. Don't ask "why." Just be curious.

Shadow work is all about approaching your feelings with curiosity. It isn't necessarily about analyzing your emotions or asking yourself why you're having certain feelings. Nor is it about labeling those feelings as good or bad, or right or wrong. Shadow work is about asking yourself questions about your emotions in order to understand and process them more effectively. What is this emotion? Does it spur any memories? If so, what are they? Do any images come to mind? If nothing comes up, that's okay. It doesn't mean you failed. The important work, and the hardest, is to allow yourself to *feel* your emotions. That is the only way through them. That is the only way to heal.

Once you begin to understand your emotions, you can begin the process of acknowledging and releasing them. This doesn't mean that the pain goes away. Nor does it mean that it will be forgotten. The goal really is to create within yourself the opportunity to confront your pain, acknowledge its existence, and say to yourself: "This does not define me. This no longer controls my life." Remember that shadow work is non-linear. The pain and emotions you are feeling will almost certainly come up again. Your journey will not take you down a direct path to a specific destination. Your feelings are going to resurface over and over. And that's normal. The key is to find ways to cope with them and to continue with your life in the best way that you can.

Sometimes people say that the painful experiences we go through in life just make us stronger. But I firmly believe that trauma does *not* make you stronger. Your difficult life experiences do *not* make you stronger. What they do is make your life difficult. And sometimes they cause lasting mental-health effects. What makes you stronger is *you*. You make yourself stronger by persisting and never giving up. You make yourself stronger by being brave enough to confront your shadow and begin the process of healing. You make yourself stronger by not allowing yourself to be defined by your life experiences. They have made you a part of who you are today, absolutely. But they do not define you. You hold the pen in your hand. You get to define who you are. You get to write the next chapter of your life.

Tools for Shadow Work

There are many tools that you can use to start you out on your healing journey. In this chapter, we'll look at a few that incorporate Anubis— including meditation, journaling, and spell work. This is not an exhaustive list, by any means, just some of the many practices that can help you in confronting your shadow.

There are several ways in which you can incorporate meditation into your shadow work. We've already discussed how daily meditations— even simple five-to-ten-minute meditations—can make you feel more grounded and balanced. Even though you may not necessarily be focused on healing, these meditations can work in conjunction with it to help you deal with the stresses of daily life and set you up to feel better overall. I find that starting my day with a quick meditation, without any kind of agenda in mind, is very helpful.

One type of meditation that can be helpful in shadow work is a meditative journey. I've already given you an example of one in chapter 11, and you'll find another at the end of this chapter. When you embark on a meditative journey, sometimes called a "vision quest," you set out in search of some kind of healing on a spiritual level. During these journeys, you may travel to your inner realm, where you discover pieces of yourself that need healing. It's important to feel grounded, safe, and protected on these journeys, and that's where Anubis can help. He often accompanies me on my meditative journeys in his role as Master Healer and Great Shaman. He acts as my protector and guardian, and he keeps me feeling safe, which is important.

Because Anubis protects the souls of both the living and the dead, he can be petitioned to do so during any kind of shamanic work, including shadow work. He is not, from my experience, an angry or vengeful deity. But, because of his role as Weigher of Souls, he should not be taken lightly. He requires high moral standards from those with whom he works. So when facing him, you must be prepared to confront the truth, however painful that may be. You must be prepared to face all aspects of yourself, even the parts you may wish to hide from the world.

But Anubis as Master Healer can also be compassionate and understanding, especially when dealing with areas related to pain and trauma. In either case, you have no reason to fear him. Respect him, but don't fear him. His role is to lead you out of the darkness of the shadow into a space of healing and light.

Journaling is another powerful tool that can be used in shadow work, because it gives you a way to "get your thoughts out," so to speak. When you write down the thoughts, feelings, and ideas that come up in your work, it makes it easier to process them. Many therapists and mental-health professionals suggest using journaling as a part of the healing process.

The nice thing about journaling is that what you write doesn't have to be coherent or organized. I love drawing on the power of free writing in my journaling. Sometimes I just need space to process my thoughts and feelings. In fact, my journal becomes a bit of a word dump at times—and, in a way, it is. But your journal can also be a place where you can put all your busy, muddy thoughts on paper and sort through them so you can get them out of your head.

Of course, magick and spells are also tools you can use in your shadow work to help you get in touch with your inner self. Since we already examined them in detail in chapter 15, I won't spend much time on them here, except to say that Anubis—as shaman, guide, and protector—can be a valuable ally as you delve deeper into your shadow. Below, I share a couple of simple spells that can be particularly useful in shadow work, because they can help to break negative energetic ties.

Simple Cord-Cutting Spell

Cord-cutting spells are used to break any energetic ties you may have with a person or a situation that is impacting you negatively. This can be someone who has had a negative influence on your life—perhaps an abuser—from whom you want to distance yourself. I have intentionally kept this spell simple, but you can add other correspondences to it if you wish. You can anoint the candles with herbs related to protection and banishment, use stones that are associated with your intention, or use different-colored candles for more specific purposes.

For this spell, you will need two black candles and a piece of twine or string. Before you start, make sure that you have the person or situation you want to address clearly in mind. Designate one candle to represent yourself and one candle to represent the person or event from whose energy you want to disconnect. As always, be sure that the surface you're working on is in a safe location to prevent fire hazards.

First, tie the piece of string around both candles, so that they are connected. Then light both candles and let them burn. As they burn, imagine yourself cutting energetic ties with the person or event in question. Imagine that they no longer have any influence over you.

When the candles have burned down to the level of the string, let the flame burn away the string connecting them. As the string burns away, say:

_____ (name of the person or event),
We are connected no more.
You have no influence over me or my life.
The damage you've done is over.
I am protected from you.

Immediately call on Anubis for protection. You may even want to perform some of the spells found in chapter 15 for an additional bit of protection to ensure that the energetic ties you are breaking do not recur.

Spell Candle to Banish Negativity

Whenever you do any kind of shadow work, it's important to shield yourself from negative energies and influences. You can do this using some of the spells offered in chapter 15, but I also recommend burning a candle dedicated to banishing negativity any time that you are doing shadow work.

To perform this spell, you will need:

- Black pillar candle large enough to be used multiple times

- Frankincense or sandalwood oil

- Mugwort

- Obsidian

Carve the shape of an ankh four times around the surface of the candle. Anoint the candle with oil, using your fingers or hands to rub the oil onto the candle. Place the candle on a surface where it can remain any time that you plan to do shadow work. Place a ring of mugwort around it and put obsidian between the carved images of the ankhs, then say this prayer:

Anubis, Shielder,
Great Protector,
Guardian and Warden,
As I light this candle,
Shield me from harm.
Wrap me in your shroud of protection.
May no negativity enter.
May none approach with ill will.

Light this candle whenever you sit with your emotions or do any kind of meditative journeying to ensure that you are protected.

Journey to Face Your Shadow

This meditative journey can be a powerful experience. If, at any point, you find it overwhelming or too painful, stop. While feeling your emotions is an important part of healing, you have to do it in a manner that is comfortable and safe. And if you don't see anything in the mirror, that's okay. Not everyone operates in the same way. It may be that your first journey is simply intended to get you into the mindset of starting down this path.

To begin, light a candle—preferably a black one, because this is a color sacred to Anubis. If you don't have a black candle, any color you have on hand will work. If music helps to put you in a relaxed state, play it.

Mentally set your intention to begin healing work and call to Anubis as shamanic healer. You can use the short prayer below, or you can write your own.

> *Anubis, Sovereign of Death,*
> *Master Healer and Lord of Night,*
> *Take my hand and guide me through the darkness*
> *With your eyes that pierce the blackness.*
> *Though afraid, I walk by your side*
> *To face my shadow,*
> *To find balance,*
> *To empower.*
> *Light my path through the darkness.*
> *Through this path, I am transformed.*

Sit comfortably in a chair or, if you prefer, lie down on your bed. If you are sitting, keep your feet flat on the floor. If you're lying down, feel the point of contact where your back and legs touch the mattress. Take as much time as you need to settle into the space, making sure that you are comfortable and relaxed. Take a few deep breaths, letting the air fill your lungs. Breathe as deeply as you can, pulling the air all the way down to your diaphragm.

Close your eyes and take a few more deep, cleansing breaths. Settle even deeper into the space you're in. Imagine there are roots growing downward through your legs and out from the bottoms of your feet into the ground beneath you. Feel them reach deep into the earth, grounding your body. Now imagine there are branches reaching up into the sky from the top of your head, connecting to the energy of the sun, the moon, and the stars. Let them uplift you. Imagine that the roots below you and the branches above you meet in the middle in your body, connecting and intertwining at your core. Take a few more deep breaths, resting in this in-between space.

You see a door in front of you. You recognize it, because you've been here before. Pause to remember what it looks like. Has anything changed about this door? Make a mental note of this, then reach for the handle and turn it. Push the door open.

Once through the door, you travel down a familiar hallway lined with torches, their warm glow filling you with a sense of calm. At the end of the hallway, you once again see the door that is decorated with patterns and the ankh. You smile, feeling a familiar energy emanating from the obsidian stone in the center.

When you pass through the door, you find yourself in a small dark room that is lit with four golden torches laden with ruby and turquoise. In the center of the room is a tall mirror, just a little taller and wider than you are. It's rather simple, but has a solid gold frame.

You sense a familiar presence in the room. Anubis is there. You see him step out of the shadows wearing a white robe with gold trim, with an ankh hanging around his neck. His presence is calming and you feel safe and protected. Before you can say anything, Anubis approaches and stands before you.

"Your road has been rough," he says. "It has not been easy, but I am proud of you for never giving up. Your strength keeps you going and has led you here to continue on your healing journey. I know that you will continue on this path and persist in seeking ways to heal and to grow."

He motions for you to follow him to the mirror. "Gaze into the mirror," he says. "Pay attention to what, or rather who, stands before you. You will see a part of you that needs healing."

"What part of me is it?" you ask.

"That, I cannot say," Anubis replies simply. "For some, it's their inner child. For some, a version of themselves lost during trauma. For others, it's the darker part of themselves that they wish to hide from the world. You need to discover for yourself what part stands before you."

You look at him apprehensively and, before you can say anything, he speaks again.

"I know this is frightening, but you needn't worry. I am here to guard and protect you. What you will see isn't another spirit or entity that can harm you. It's a reflection of yourself." He gives your arm a gentle squeeze.

You turn toward the mirror and take a few deep breaths. Gazing into it, you see something begin to appear. Pay attention to it. What do you see? What do you look like here? How old are you? Are there any other details that you can make out? Spend some time with this part of yourself. Don't rush it. Take as much time as you need.

When you are ready, speak what you wish to say to yourself. Be open and honest. This may be painful, as it may involve memories, thoughts, and feelings that are difficult to acknowledge. Remember that Anubis is there with you and that you are safe.

Invite this part of yourself to return with you through the mirror. If it agrees, take its hand and help it. If not, don't force it. That's okay. Maybe that part of you isn't ready. You can always come back to this space and try again. Anubis will be here to guard and protect you during these journeys to rediscover the parts of you that need healing.

Before you leave, Anubis has a message for you. You turn to him and listen as he speaks. What does he say? Listen carefully to his message. Take note of it in your mind so you can remember it later.

When you feel that you are finished, thank Anubis and go back through the door. Take a deep breath and retrace your steps down the corridor. As you walk, recall the words Anubis spoke to you and the experience you had with the mirror. When you reach your personal door, go through it and close it behind you.

Pause for a moment and take several deep breaths. With each one, let yourself become aware of your body and your surroundings. Wiggle your fingers and your toes. Move your head. Begin to stretch a little. Finally, open your eyes.

Drink some water and eat the snack that you prepared, fully returning yourself back into your physical body. In your journal, write what you remember about your experience, including as many details as you can and paying close attention to what Anubis told you. What did you see? What did you feel? What thoughts or ideas came up? You may also want to write down anything you want to accomplish on your healing journey as you move forward. Remember, the act of writing can be cathartic.

You can perform this meditation whenever it meets your own personal needs, which may change from session to session. Don't push yourself to feel that you have healing "deadlines" to meet. Healing has parts that are intentional, but it should also happen at a pace that fits you.

Journal Prompts

- Have you previously done any kind of shadow work? If so, what has it looked like for you? If not, what areas of your life need attention?

- How can you include Anubis in your shadow work?

CHAPTER 18

Formal Dedication

"Walk with me, dearest child, and I will lead you down the path that leads to the secrets and the mysteries of the world—seen and unseen. On this journey, you will shed what no longer serves you and grow into the best version of yourself that you can be. Painful as it may be at times, take my hand, and I will guide you, shielding and protecting you from harm. Take my hand, and I will teach you the ways of magick and of divination known only to those willing to practice and learn. We will travel to the realm of spirits, where I will teach you how to commune with the dead and walk with ancestors. I will lead you to become a guardian for those who need protection and a guide to those who are lost. Join me, in this space of light and shadow."

ANUBIS TO ME DURING A MEDITATION

The decision to dedicate yourself formally to Anubis is a highly personal one made between you and him. It entails making a formal promise to include him as an integral part of your life and to dedicate your time and energy to him in some way. This promise can take different forms for different people, but it essentially comes down to creating a lasting bond between you.

One type of formal dedication is to adopt a god or goddess as a patron deity. This isn't a new practice. In fact, entire cities in the ancient world had patron deities. Athens had Athena. Thebes had Amun (or Amun-Ra). Memphis had Ptah. Today, practitioners across many faiths have a patron deity or saint to whom they dedicate themselves, and they spend much of their practice in service to them. Many Pagans, witches, and Kemetics who work with gods in some way dedicate themselves to patron deities, making them the central focus of their practice. They may include statues or representations of them on their main altars and spend much of their time working with them.

A formal dedication can also consist of some act of service, as in the priesthood. Becoming a priest or priestess is a sacred act that can take years of learning, study, and teaching. It's not a decision to be taken lightly, and it's certainly not for everyone. Being a priest can include leading ceremonies and rituals, but it can also be a formal commitment to teaching, writing, and sharing. This generally entails becoming more of a public figure or assuming a public role.

Some dedicate themselves to being scholars, in which case they spend their time delving into the mysteries of their chosen deity. As a scholar of Anubis, I spend a lot of my time researching, reading, and exploring books and materials about him, as well as writing about him for a number of different audiences.

Of course, you may decide to incorporate any of these elements into your dedication to Anubis. And how you choose to dedicate yourself to him need not be limited to one specific thing. It's highly personal and should be shaped by what you and he decide to do going forward. There is no right or wrong answer.

Deciding whether or not to dedicate yourself formally to Anubis is not something you should take lightly. I strongly encourage you to stop and really think about it. Write out your thoughts in your journal. If you decide to go forward, it can really enhance your life. But it isn't always easy. Formal dedication comes with its own set of challenges, including accountability and responsibility.

The Mantle of Anubis

When you take on the mantle of Anubis, you commit yourself to facing the darker aspects of life and bringing them into the light. Anubis is the Lord of Transformation. When you dedicate yourself to him, you declare yourself willing to accept change and transformation where it is needed. You agree to do the difficult work needed to make these changes. You accept the reponsibility of being brave and facing your fears and insecurities. You promise to become a more confident, balanced person and the best version of yourself that you can be. Life isn't always sunshine and rainbows, but being brave and dealing with its challenges is something that is much easier with Anubis by your side.

When you decide to form a lasting connection to Anubis, you commit to spending time deepening your relationship with him. This is a highly personal process that can include some of the ideas mentioned above, but it may also include other elements that fit best with your own experience and your own spirituality. There are four important steps to follow as you begin your journey: *Be certain. Be clear. Be realistic. Plan carefully.*

First, be certain that you want to go down this path. I know this sounds silly, but it's important to make sure that this is something you really want to do and that you're going to commit to doing. Making promises that you don't keep to a god whose task it is to weigh souls is not something you should do.

Once you have confirmed your commitment, decide in what capacity you want to serve Anubis. Are you interested in him as your patron deity? Do you want him as the core focus of your spiritual practice? Are you interested in diving deeper—to learning, writing, and sharing? Do you want to serve others and become a priest? It's entirely up to you the kind of relationship you have with Anubis; just be clear about what that is. I highly recommend consulting tarot or oracle cards to gain some insight that can help you make your decision.

Next, be realistic about how much time you're going to dedicate to your practice. Becoming a priest of Anubis doesn't mean that you suddenly become a monk who spends every hour of every day honoring and serving him, just as becoming an author or a blogger doesn't mean that you have to quit your day job to write. Life circumstances change, and you may be able to spend more time with him at certain times of the year than others. And that's okay. Just be sure that you consider these issues ahead of time. It may be helpful, at least initially, to lay out in advance just how often and when you plan to work with Anubis. As time passes and you gain more experience, you may not need this more structured approach.

Finally, I think it's a good idea to plan your dedication carefully. Decide what you are going to wear, what you want to include on your altar, and what you will do during your ritual. Decide what correspondences you want to include on your altar, even down to the color of the candles and the types of stones you'll use, if any.

Here are some ideas to get you going:

- Wear black clothes. These don't have to be robes or anything special. But, because black is a color sacred to Anubis as a color of protection, magick, and transformation, it's a good choice.

- Decide if you will wear any jewelry or amulets. An ankh or another symbol of Anubis can be appropriate, if you have one.

- Try to use white and/or black candles. I like to include one of each.

- Consider using stones like smoky quartz, jet, onyx, obsidian, clear quartz, or black tourmaline. Alternatively, choose stones that go with your intuition and that call to you.

- Write out what you plan to say in your ritual. You can speak spontaneously, but, at the very minimum, decide what you are going to say. The last thing you want to do is to ramble on or make promises that you aren't going to keep. I am all for authenticity in the moment—it's how I operate most of the time. But I think there's also a time and a place for a more formalized approach. Writing out what you want to say in advance can help ensure that you include everything you want to and don't miss anything important.

Here's an example of a written intent, but you can also write one of your own that reflects your own personal spiritual goals:

Hail Anubis, Lord of Death!
Guide me through transformation.
Hail Anubis, Master of Secrets!
Teach me the hidden knowledge.
Hail Anubis, Great Shaman!
Guide me to my inner realms.
Hail Anubis, Great Guardian!
Shroud me in your cloak of protection.
I dedicate myself to you,
To learning from and about you,
To deepening our connection,
And to doing the work.
With you as my companion,
I seek to guide, to heal, to transform, and to learn.
Hail Anubis, Keeper of Keys!
Grant me my key.
Hail Anubis, Pharaoh of the Underworld!
Usher me down my path.
Hail Anubis, Celestial One!
Lead me through the stars.
Hail Anubis, Liminal Lord!
Sit with me in the space between light and shadow.

Receiving the Mantle of Anubis

The following is a ritual you can use to dedicate yourself to the service of Anubis. To perform it, you will need:

- An offering of your choosing

- Incense

- Nine stones of your choosing (a combination of clear quartz, jet, obsidian, black tourmaline, and smoky quartz)

- One black candle

- One white candle

- Statue or artwork of Anubis

Prepare your altar space and place the statue of Anubis between the two candles, with the black candle on the right and the white candle on the left. Place the offering and incense on the altar.

Prepare your body using the ritual bath described in chapter 15, dressing yourself in appropriate clothes, and adorning yourself with any amulets or jewelry you have decided to wear (if any). Sit or kneel at your altar space, if that is comfortable for you. If it's not, you can perform the ritual standing.

Place the nine stones in a circle that encompasses you and your altar space, trying to keep them equidistant from each other. Close your eyes and imagine that the nine stones are forming a protective barrier around you and the altar. Imagine that their energies connect and extend around you and above you, forming a protective dome. Imagine this dome as an impenetrable force field.

Invite Anubis to be present using the words below. As you invoke him, light the two candles, in any order.

Anubis, Lord of Death and Transformation,
Great Protector and Guardian,
Healer and Master of Secrets and Mysteries,
Great Liminal Lord,
Celestial One of Magick,
I invite you here into this space now.
I ask you to be with me during this ritual.
I ask for your presence, your protection, and your guidance.
I present myself here to dedicate myself to you.

Light the incense and let it burn as you continue. Then state your written intention to Anubis.

Now it is time to journey to receive the mantle of Anubis.

Sit comfortably in your chair, with your feet flat on the floor. If you prefer to stand, distribute your weight evenly on your feet to ground yourself. Take a few moments to let yourself "wiggle" into a comfortable position, letting yourself fully relax. Take three deep breaths, letting the air fill your lungs and pulling it down to your diaphragm. Close your eyes and take three more deep breaths, letting your body settle even more.

Imagine there are roots growing downward through your legs and out from the bottoms of your feet into the ground beneath you. Feel them reach deep into the earth, grounding your body into the space. Imagine there are branches emerging from the top of your head and reaching up into the sky, connecting to the energy of the sun, the moon, and the stars. Let them uplift you. Then imagine that the roots below you and the branches above you meet in the middle of your body, connecting and intertwining at your core. Take a few more deep breaths, resting in this in-between space.

Rest in this liminal space for a moment, allowing yourself to deepen into this meditative state. Feel yourself sinking deeper, your soul almost freeing itself from your body. With each breath, you feel more and more weightless and free. You are completely rested within this space.

Return to the personal door you passed through the first time you met Anubis. By now, it should look familiar. You recognize it and know immediately that this is your door—the door to your inner world.

You enter the door and travel down the familiar hallway lined with torches. The torches provide a warm glow that makes you smile. You run your fingers across the smooth, cool sand-colored blocks on the wall. At the end of the hallway, you see the door with the swirling patterns and the ankh, with the obsidian in the center. You smile, feeling its familiar energy.

When you pass through the door, you find yourself in a large room whose walls and floor of sand-colored stone remind you of the hallway. Torches line the walls, and a high ceiling seems to reach up and up.

In the center of the room, you see an altar table with a single black candle on it, similar to the one that was there when you first met Anubis. There is an ankh carved on its side, along with the hieroglyph for Anpu. Next to the candle is a folded black cloth of some kind. A sweet, musky, spicy incense is burning on the other side of the candle. The aroma fills the air and gives you a sense of calm, but it also fills the air with a feeling of magick and mystery.

The candle lights, and you feel a familiar presence in the room. Anubis, Lord of Death, steps out from the shadows wearing a golden garment around his waist, a golden mantle around his shoulders and neck, and a pharaoh's ceremonial headpiece. You can see his dark skin. His golden eyes shine, reminding you of the light within the darkness that rests within the Liminal Lord.

"Welcome back," he says to you with a smile. "Come." He motions you to come closer. You approach and stand before him.

State your intention to him. Tell him what you wish to express to him, what kind of relationship you'd like to build, and what kind of dedication you'd like to make to him. Be open and honest; speak from the heart.

He responds to what you say. What does he say to you? Take note of everything he says.

"It's time, then," he says, reaching for the cloth on the table. As he unfolds it and holds it up, you see that it is a shroud. He puts it around your shoulders, and it drapes around you. You see that it is black with gold trim. You immediately feel its energy, *his* energy, surrounding you and within you. It's invigorating, but also calming, protective, and grounding.

Anubis takes a small bowl from the altar that looks as if it is filled with oil. He dabs his thumb into the oil. You can smell its fragrant scent of sandalwood, pine, and frankincense. He reaches toward your forehead and draws the shape of an ankh on it. He utters some words in a language that you do not understand, and you feel that same energy move through you again in waves. You take a few deep breaths. Feeling calm and centered, you know that it is done.

"We are now bonded," he says. "I am with you to protect you, to guide you, and to teach you. But never forget that or take it for granted." You make a mental note of that.

Ask Anubis any questions that you wish now. Take note of anything that he says to you.

"Thank you, dear one. I look forward to our connection," he says before you leave.

When you are ready, you thank him and turn toward the door. Before you pass through it, you look back. He raises his hand in farewell, then disappears as the candle goes out. You take a deep breath, go through the door, and retrace your steps down the corridor. As you walk, you recall the experience you just went through. You remind yourself of the mantle that you wear and the promise that you made. When you reach your personal door, you pass through it and close it behind you.

Pause for a moment and take several deep breaths. With each breath, let yourself become aware of your body and your surroundings. Wiggle your fingers and your toes. Move your head. Begin to stretch a little. Finally, open your eyes.

Drink some water and eat the snack that you prepared, fully returning yourself back into your physical body.

Place your offering on your altar and say:

> *Liminal Lord of Light and Shadow,*
> *I offer this _____ (name your offering) to you as a promise*
> *That I will dedicate myself to you.*
> *I proudly wear the shroud you gave me.*
> *May our connection grow and deepen.*
> *Dua Anpu!*

In your journal, write what you remember from the journey, including as many details as you can and paying close attention to what Anubis told you. Spend some time meditating and reflecting. Then note down any other important thoughts that come up.

When you are finished, imagine that the energy bubble around you recedes back into the stones. You can remove them from the circle at this time.

As you extinguish the candles, thank Anubis for being present by saying:

> *Hail to the Obsidian God of Death!*
> *Hail Anubis!*

Dispose of your offering in a proper manner (see chapter 13).

Journal Prompts

- Spend time recording everything about your dedication ritual. Write down the things you included, the steps, and the process. Record anything that Anubis said to you. Include how you felt, the things you saw, and anything else that came up during your journey.

- Record your written intent for later reference and to mark the importance of it.

- How do you plan to put your dedication into action? What will you do?

Conclusion

Toward the end of the recent pandemic, my partner and I took many weekend trips to get away from the busyness of life, relax, and spend time in nature. It had been a rough few years, what with the pandemic and its financial impacts, and some new health concerns that took up a lot of my physical and mental energy. I was feeling rather disconnected from the world around me and from the gods and spirits in my life.

We spent Samhain at a mountain resort. It was off-season and there weren't many tourists around because of the cold temperatures. I, on the other hand, find the cold to be quite invigorating. It's a stark reminder that I am alive, and I feel that to the depths of my soul. After an evening sitting by the lake and gazing at the stars and the moon, we returned to our hotel and sat out on the patio, which faced an open field between the hotel and the lake. A few minutes later, a coyote appeared. While he didn't approach us, he didn't seem to be afraid of us. He just sat there in the moonlight and watched us, then trotted off.

Two weeks later, we were hiking along the coast in northern California and we decided to save time and our tiring legs and feet by taking a "shortcut" to get back to the car. Our GPS told us there was a path, but it was overgrown with tall grass and weeds.

As we trekked along the path, something caught my eye in the distance. Another coyote! Of course, I immediately thought of Anubis and the experience I had had those many years ago with my grandfather.

We watched silently. The coyote was watching something intently in the grass, clearly ready to pounce. A moment later, it leapt into the air, dove down into the grass, and caught its prey. Then it trotted off.

Throughout my life, I've seen coyotes at times when I least expected to, reminding me that, no matter where I go, no matter what I do, no matter what is happening in my life, Anubis is there by my side. And I find eternal comfort in that.

Anubis is a complex and powerful deity who resides in more spaces than you can imagine—in the sands of Egypt, in the cities of Europe, and in the noisy bustle of our modern lives. He stands today as an icon for all things magickal and for the mysteries of life and death. Even those who are not Pagans, witches, or Kemetics recognize him.

As Lord of Death and Pharaoh of the Underworld, he teaches us that death is not the end, but the beginning as well. He shows us that the changes we go through in life can lead us to places we need to go, even if they are uncomfortable. As the Lord of Transformation and Great Shaman, he acts as a powerful ally in this kind of work.

As Master of Mysteries, Anubis teaches us the lessons learned from death. As Master of Secrets, he reveals deep wisdom and knowledge through magick, divination, and mediumship. As Great Protector, he is there for everyone, regardless of who they are or where they come from. He has a particular soft spot for the lost and the marginalized, but every soul is worthy of his protection.

As Weigher of Souls, he reminds us to live our lives with integrity and to speak and live our truth. As the Celestial One, he reminds us that themes of death and magick rest in the sun, the moon, and the stars, as well as in the earth and the Underworld. They persist across all dimensions of time and space.

No matter how you see Anubis or how you approach him, I wish you all the best in building your relationship with him. Don't forget that, when life gets hard, he will always be there, watching from the shadows, ready to bring light into the darkness.

APPENDIX A

Historical Timeline of Ancient Egypt

- **Approximately 5500 BCE:** Nomadic farmers began settling around the fertile lands of the Nile delta, known as the "black lands" ("Kemet" in the ancient Egyptian language).

- **3400–3100 BCE:** Two kingdoms were well established—Upper Egypt (southern highlands) and Lower Egypt (northern lowlands of the Nile delta). The hieroglyphic writing system was well established by this point.

- **Approximately 3100 BCE:** A king (either Menes or Narmer) united the two kingdoms of Egypt and became pharaoh of the First Dynasty.

- **2686–2181 BCE:** Known as the Old Kingdom, a Golden Age. This was a time of prosperity heavily focused on expansion and economic growth. The famous pyramids at Giza were built. The king during this time was seen as a central figure and was held in great respect. The overuse of natural resources and forced labor caused unrest and turmoil in the country. Temples and local authority figures no longer felt compelled to pay tribute to the king, which led to bankruptcy. The nation was yet again divided into more than one kingdom.

- **2055–1650 BCE:** Known as the Middle Kingdom. Egypt was again united into one kingdom. More power was granted to local governments. Artistry, craftsmanship, and literature flourished. Trade with nearby nations was expanded.

- **1650–1550 BCE:** A group known as the Hyksos, who were most likely of Western Semitic, Levantine derivation, ruled Egypt, likely having entered slowly by peaceful means in the years prior, but then taking over by force. They brought with them horses, chariots, and new military tactics that would forever transform Egypt.

- **1550–1069 BCE:** Known as the New Kingdom, another Golden Age. The Hyksos were defeated. The borders of Egypt were expanded south into what is now Sudan and northeast into what is now called the Middle East. More power and economic prosperity were shared with local authorities rather than resting solely with the king. Akhenaten attempted to ban the worship of all deities except Aten until his death, when this attempt at monotheism crumbled. The famous boy king Tutankhamun ruled from 1336 to 1327 BCE. There was a rise in tomb raiding.

- **1069–747 BCE:** A time of change in power. Libyans, Assyrians, and Nubians all fought for conquest of Egypt, and its rule changed hands multiple times. The land was once again divided.

- **747–332 BCE:** Known as the Late Period. An attempt at reuniting Egypt and re-establishing power occurred around 747 BCE and lasted until 525 BCE. Persians conquered Egypt in 525 BCE and annexed it as one of its territories. It remained a territory of Persia until 404 BCE.

- **332 BCE:** After Alexander the Great defeated the Persians, he was recognized as pharaoh of Egypt until his death in 323 BCE.

- **305–30 BCE:** Known as the Ptolemaic Dynasty, after Ptolemy I Soter, who was a general in Alexander the Great's army. Ptolemy was among the foremost of the Diadochi, the rival generals, relatives, and friends of Alexander who sought to rule his vast empire after his death. Ptolemy captured Egypt and ruled it as pharaoh, as did his descendants.

- **51–30 BCE:** The rise of Cleopatra VII, last pharaoh of Egypt. Powerful and determined, Cleopatra endured a series of conquests in order to maintain her rule over Egypt and retain its independence. Eventually, she ended her own life as a way to avoid surrendering to Octavian of Rome.

- **30–27 BCE:** Octavian of Rome declared himself as the first Roman Emperor, thus beginning the Roman Empire. He ruled under the title Augustus Caesar.

APPENDIX B

List of Correspondences

There are many animals, objects, and elements associated with Anubis. Some of those listed below come from historical records; some come from my personal experience. You may come across others that are not included in this list. Feel free to add them to your journal.

- **Animals:** jackal, dog, wolf, coyote, fox, leopard

- **Colors:** black, gold, brown, gray, white

- **Day:** Saturday

- **Holidays and celebrations:** summer and winter solstice, dog days, Scorpio season, spring and autumn equinoxes

- **Incense:** cedarwood, sandalwood, frankincense, myrrh, pine, kyphi

- **Number:** 8

- **Planets and aspects:** Pluto, Chiron, Mercury, Anubis asteroid (#1912)

- **Plants:** rosemary, yarrow, blackberry/bramble, sage, mugwort

- **Stones:** obsidian, black tourmaline, hematite, smoky quartz, jet, amethyst, lapis lazuli

- **Symbols:** ankh, pyramid, bones, skull, staff, keys, scales, mummies, bandage wrappings, gravestone, Eye of Horus, sarcophagus, dogs

- **Trees:** cedar, yew, cypress, elm, pine, acacia, baobab, redwood

- **Zodiac:** Libra, Scorpio

APPENDIX C

Index of Prayers and Practices

Chapter 16

Chapter 17

Chapter 18

Bibliography

Books

Allen, James P. *The Art of Medicine in Ancient Egypt*. New York: The Metropolitan Museum of Art, 2005–6.

Betz, Hans Dieter. *The Greek Magical Papyri in Translation, Including the Demotic Spells*, 2nd Edition. Chicago, IL: The University of Chicago Press, 1996.

Budge, E. A. Wallis. *The Gods of the Egyptians: Studies in Egyptian Mythology*, Vol 1. New York: Dover Publications, 2016.

——————. *The Gods of the Egyptians: Studies in Egyptian Mythology*, Vol 2. New York, NY: Dover Publications, 2014.

——————. *Legends of the Egyptian Gods: Hieroglyphic Texts and Translations*. New York: Dover Publications, 2018.

Campbell, Joseph. *The Hero with a Thousand Faces*, 3rd Ed. Novato, CA: New World Library, 2012.

Clark, Rosemary. *Sacred Magic of Egypt*. St. Paul, MN: Llewellyn, 2003.

David, Rosalie. *Handbook to Life in Ancient Egypt*, Revised Edition. New York: Facts on File, Inc., 2003.

DuQuesne, Terence. "A Coptic Initiatory Invocation (PGM IV 1–25): an essay in interpretation with critical text, translation, and commentary." In *Oxfordshire Communications in Egyptology II*. London: Darengo, 1994.

——————. "At the Court of Osiris." In *Oxfordshire Communications in Egyptology IV*. Thame, Oxfordshire: Darengo, 1991.

——————. "Anubis." In *The Encyclopedia of Ancient History*, First Edition (eds. R. S. Bagnall, K. Brodersen, C. B. Champion, A. Erskine and S. R. Huebner). Hoboken, NJ: Wiley-Blackwell, 2013.

——————. "Jackal at the Shaman's Gate." In *Oxfordshire Communications in Egyptology III*. Thame, Oxfordshire: Darengo, 1991.

Edgar Allen Poe Complete Tales and Poems. New York: Fall River Press, 2012.

Gaiman, Neil. *American Gods*. New York: Harper Collins, 2001.

Goelet Jr., Ogden, Raymond Faulkner, Carol R. Andrews, J. Daniel Gunther, and James Wasserman. *The Egyptian Book of the Dead: The Book of Going Forth by Day: The Complete Papyrus of Ani Featuring Integrated Text and Full-Color Images.* San Francisco: Chronicle Books, 2015.

Griffith, F. L. and Herbert Thompson. *Leyden Papyrus: An Egyptian Magical Book.* New York, NY: Dover Publications, 1974.

Hawking, Stephen in a speech at the 2012 Paralympic Games in London, United Kingdom, 2012.

Illes, Judika. *Encyclopedia of Spirits: The Ultimate Guide to the Magic of Fairies, Genies, Demons, Ghosts, Gods, and Goddesses.* New York: HarperOne, 2009.

Kynes, Sandra. *Llewellyn's Complete Book of Correspondences: A Comprehensive and Cross-Referenced Resource for Pagans and Wiccans.* Woodbury, MN: Llewellyn, 2018.

Marman, Doug. *It Is What It Is: The Personal Discourses of Rumi.* Ridgefield, WA: Spiritual Dialogues Project, 2010.

Mertz, Barbara. *Red Land, Black Land: Daily Life in Ancient Egypt.* New York: Harper Collins, 2008. pp. 115–118.

Miller, Madeline. *Circe.* New York: Back Bay Books, 2020.

———. *The Song of Achilles.* New York: HarperCollins, 2012.

Osbon, Diane K. ed. *Reflections on the Art of Living: A Joseph Campbell Companion.* New York: HarperCollins, 1991.

Page, Judith and Jan A. Malique. *Pathworking with the Egyptian Gods.* Woodbury, MN: Llewellyn, 2010.

Pinch, Geraldine. *Egyptian Mythology: A Guide to the Gods, Goddesses, and Traditions of Ancient Egypt.* New York: Oxford University Press, 2002.

Price, Campbell, Roger Forshaw, Andrew Chamberlain, Paul Nicholson, Robert Morkot, and Joyce Tyldesley, eds. *Mummies, Magic, and Medicine in Ancient Egypt: Multidisciplinary Essays for Rosalie David.* Manchester: Manchester University Press, 2016.

Riordan, Rick. *The Red Pyramid.* New York: Disney-Hyperion, 2010.

Shecter, Vicky Alvear. *Anubis Speaks! A Guide to the Afterlife.* Honesdale, PA: Boyds Mills Press, 2013.

Strudwick, Helen, ed. *The Encyclopedia of Ancient Egypt.* New York: Metro Books, 2006.

Wilfong, T. G. *Death Dogs: The Jackal Gods of Ancient Egypt.* Ann Arbor, MI: Kelsey Museum of Archaeology, 2015.

Wilkinson, Richard H. *The Complete Gods and Goddesses of Ancient Egypt.* London: Thames & Hudson, 2003.

Internet

9-8-8 Lifeline. 9-8-8 Suicide and Crisis Lifeline. 2023. *988lifeline.org.*

"ANKH—Egyptian Symbol of Life." National Park Service, November 5, 2015. *nps.gov.*

Hill, J. "Kyphi." Ancient Egypt Online, 2009. *ancientegyptonline.co.uk.*

Kamrin, Janice. "Telling Time in Ancient Egypt: Essay: The Metropolitan Museum of Art: Heilbrunn Timeline of Art History." The Met's Heilbrunn Timeline of Art History, February 2017. *metmuseum .org.*

Meehan, Evan. "Anubis." Mythopedia, November 29, 2022. *mytho pedia.com.*

NPR Staff. "Millions of Mummified Dogs Found in Ancient Egyptian Catacombs." NPR, July 4, 2015. *npr.org.*

Smith, Moya. "Anubis." Western Australian Museum, 2013. *museum .wa.gov.au.*

Stünkel, Isabel. "The Human Connection: Photographs from Tutankhamun's Tomb." The Metropolitan Museum of Art, March 1, 2023. *metmuseum.org.*

The Griffith Institute Staff. "Kemet." The Griffith Institute. *griffith .ox.ac.uk.*

Wolfenoot. *wolfenoot.com.*

Periodicals

Bede Millard, Dom. "St. Christopher and the Lunar Disc of Anubis." *The Journal of Egyptian Archaeology* 73 (1987): 223–238.

DuQuesne, Terence. "Jmjwt." In Willeke Wendrich (ed.), *UCLA Encyclopedia of Egyptology.* Los Angeles: UCLA, January 1, 2012. *digital2.library.ucla.edu.*

Gaber, Amr. "A Case of Divine Adultery Investigated." *Journal of the American Research Center in Egypt* 51 (2015): 303–328.

Ritner, Robert K. "Anubis and the Lunar Disc." *The Journal of Egyptian Archaeology* 71 (1985): 149–55.

Stefanovic, Daniejela. "The 'Christianisation' of Hermanubis." *Historia: Zeitschrift für Alte Geschichte* (62): 506–155.

Art Credits

p. xiv. Statuette of Anubis. Ptolemaic Period. 332–30 BCE. In the collection of the Metropolitan Museum of Art, New York.

p. 16. Anubis the jackal. *iStock.com*

p. 17. Statue of Anubis depicting him in human form with the head of a black canid. *iStock.com*.

p. 18. The Anubis Shrine in situ at the entrance of the Treasury of King Tut's Tomb (Tomb KV 62), Valley of the Kings. A digital reproduction of a 1922 photograph by Harry Burton (1879–1940). Frank Miesnikowicz / Alamy Stock Photo.

p. 20. Hieroglyph that represents the name Anubis. From the collection of the author.

p. 23. The King Haremhab with Anubis, Tomb of Haremhab, circa 1323–1295 BCE. In the collection of the Metropolitan Museum of Art, New York.

p. 30. Anubis and Set. Based on New Kingdom tomb paintings. Jeff Dahl, CC BY-SA 4.0, via Wikimedia Commons.

p. 38. Osiris and Anubis. Detail of the frieze of the wells in the tomb of Pharaoh Horemheb, showing the gods Osiris, Anubis, and Horus. Horemheb was the last pharaoh of the XVIIIth Dynasty. Jean-Pierre Dalbéra, CC BY 2.0, via Wikimedia Commons.

p. 47. This wooden statue (664-30 BCE) depicts Anubis poised and ready to defend a burial site, guarding the necropolis, one of his commonest roles. In this role, Anubis closely resembles a full-bodied jackal. Charles Edwin Wilbour Fund. Brooklyn Museum. CC BY 3.0.

p. 47. Priests of Anubis, the guide of the dead and the god of tombs and embalming, perform the opening of the mouth ritual. Extract from the Papyrus of Hunefer, a 19th-Dynasty Book of the Dead (c. 1300 BCE). From the Book of the Dead of Hunefer. Hunefer, Public domain, via Wikimedia Commons.

p. 48. A relief depicting the god Anubis attending to the mummy of a worker, identified as either Amennakht or Nebenmaat. The relief, and the tomb it is in, date to the reign of Ramesses II (1279–1213 BCE). From the necropolis at Deir el-Medina. Thebes, Egypt. This image was first published on Flickr. Original image by Jean Robert Thibault. Uploaded by Arienne King, published on September 4, 2020. The copyright holder has published this content under the following license: Creative Commons Attribution-ShareAlike, via Wikimedia Commons.

p. 53. Ra traveling through the underworld in his barque, from the copy of the Book of Gates in the tomb of Ramses I (Tomb KV16), circa 1290 BCE. Book_of_Gates_Barque_of_Ra.jpg: derivative work: A. Parrot, public domain, via Wikimedia Commons.

p. 58. From the Book of the Dead of Hunefer. Hunefer (c. 1275 BCE) depicts the jackal-headed Anubis weighing a heart against the feather of truth on the scale of Maat, while ibis-headed Thoth records the result. Having a heart equal to the weight of the feather allows passage to the afterlife, whereas an imbalance results in a meal for Ammit, the chimera of crocodile, lion, and hippopotamus. Circa 1275 BCE. Hunefer, public domain, via Wikimedia Commons.

p. 59. Anubis Weighing the Heart, Tomb of Nakhtamun
New Kingdom, Ramesside. Circa 1279–1213 BCE (Nina de Garis Davies). In the collection of the Metropolitan Museum of Art, New York.

p. 76. Shabti of Yuya. New Kingdom. Circa 1390–1352 BCE. As the parents of Queen Tiye, wife of Amenhotep III, Yuya and Tjuyu were granted burial in the Valley of the Kings. On view at The Met Fifth Avenue in Gallery 119.

p. 80. Anubis as defender of Dionysus. Circa A.D. 2nd–3rd century. Elements from Egyptian and Greek mythology are combined in this figure. Anubis is represented, wearing military costume and breastplate that signify his role as a fighter against the enemies of Dionysus with whom the Greeks equated Osiris. From the collection of the Metropolitan Museum of Art, New York.

p. 82. left. Anubis, Hermes or Thot: Mystic Procession: Egyptian Religious Symbols and Tableaux Engraving Antique Illustration, Published 1851. *istock.com.*

p. 82, right. Hermanubis marble statue, 1st–2nd century CE (Vatican Museums). © User:Colin / Wikimedia Commons.

p. 83. The king Rameses hand in hand with Anubis, the jackal-headed god of the underworld and, to the left the falcon-headed god Horus, wearing the double crown of Upper and Lower Egypt. From the chamber of the tomb of Rameses I (Tomb KV16). 1292–1290 BCE. Leon Petrosyan, CC BY-SA 4.0, via Wikimedia Commons.

p. 84. Amulet of Wepwawet. Middle Kingdom, ca. 1850–1775 BCE. From the collection at the Metropolitan Museum of Art, New York.

p. 85. Hekate, 6th century BCE. Museum der Universität Tübingen, *http://www.theoi.com/Gallery/T16.5.html,* public domain, via Wikimedia Commons.

p. 106. The tarot Judgment card, one often associated with Anubis. From the collection of the author.

p. 113. Ritual statue of Anubis. *iStock.com.*

p. 138. Altar to Anubis containing statues, stones, and crystals. From the collection of the author.

About the Author

Charlie Larson, MA, has been a practicing witch and eclectic Pagan for over two decades. He holds both a bachelor's and a master's degree in linguistics and has been a writer and educator for most of his adult life. Charlie is passionate about nature, ancestral magick, energy healing, and shadow work. He is a priest of Anubis and works closely with Hekate and other deities. A leader in his coven since the 2000s, he has written and taught in various online communities since 2016. He currently resides in California. You can connect with Charlie at *anubislightandshadow.com.*

To Our Readers

Weiser Books, an imprint of Red Wheel/Weiser, publishes books across the entire spectrum of occult, esoteric, speculative, and New Age subjects. Our mission is to publish quality books that will make a difference in people's lives without advocating any one particular path or field of study. We value the integrity, originality, and depth of knowledge of our authors.

Our readers are our most important resource, and we appreciate your input, suggestions, and ideas about what you would like to see published.

Visit our website at *www.redwheelweiser.com*, where you can learn about our upcoming books and free downloads, and also find links to sign up for our newsletter and exclusive offers.

You can also contact us at *info@rwwbooks.com* or at

Red Wheel/Weiser, LLC
65 Parker Street, Suite 7
Newburyport, MA 01950